UNL

THE
MYSTERY
OF YOUR
EMOTIONS

BOOKS BY ARCHIBALD D. HART

Adrenalin and Stress

Children and Divorce

*Coping with Depression in the Ministry and Other Helping
Professions*

Counseling the Depressed

15 Principles for Achieving Happiness

Overcoming Anxiety

UNLOCKING THE MYSTERY OF YOUR EMOTIONS

ARCHIBALD D. HART, Ph.D

WORD PUBLISHING
Dallas · London · Sydney · Singapore

UNLOCKING THE MYSTERY OF YOUR EMOTIONS

Formerly published as *Feeling Free* by Fleming H. Revell Company

Copyright © 1979, 1989 by Archibald D. Hart

Scripture quotations identified KJV are based on the King James Version of the Bible.
Scripture quotations identified NEB are from the New English Bible. © The Delegates of the Oxford University Press and the Syndics of the Cambridge University Press 1961 and 1970. Reprinted by permission.
Excerpt from *The Velveteen Rabbit* by Margery Williams. Reprinted by permission of Doubleday & Company Inc.

Library of Congress Cataloging in Publication Data

Hart, Archibald D
  Feeling free.

  Includes bibliographical references and index.
  1. Emotions.   2. Psychology—Popular works.
3. Christian life—1960–   I. Title.
BF561.H38 152.4 78-26474
ISBN 0-8499-3199-1

  01239 BKC 98765432

Printed in the United States of America

TO
Those who have helped me find my freedom
and become real:

Kathleen, my understanding and patient wife;

Catherine, Sharon, and *Sylvia,*
three daughters tolerant of a father's many shortcomings
and faithful in their love

Contents

List of Figures

Introduction

The greatest battle the self must wage is against the emotions. The surest sign of maturity is the ability to experience one's emotions freely and integrate them into all aspects of one's being.

Feelings are an essential part of life. You cannot escape them and they need to be received as gifts from God. For many, however, the emotions represent pain and failure. Believe me, the pain of the mind is just as great as the pain of the body.

If you are confused about your emotions and cannot make sense out of your feelings, this book is for you. If you are human, you are likely to be having trouble with your emotions in one of two ways—either you will be overwhelmed by them, or you will have found a way to overcontrol them.

If you are afraid of your emotions, it is probably because you neither understand them nor can you control them. You sense, rather, that *they* control you. Anger, hate, depression, guilt, jealousy, and the like have imprisoned you. There is nothing you seem to be able to do to free yourself from their grip once they have hold of you.

If you are a male, it is highly probable that, rather than being imprisoned by your emotions, you have imprisoned them. From your earliest years you have learned to keep your emotions under tight control. You have been taught that it is weak to be emotional: "Crying is for sissies. Strong men can take everything that is dished out and never flinch." The result is, of course, that now you can't feel at all. Anesthetized to all emotions, you have built a cast-iron protective system that will withstand any emotional onslaught. You have imprisoned your emotions, but in the process have imprisoned yourself.

Which is better—to be overcontrolling of your feelings or to be controlled by them? In this book I seek to explore this issue carefully. I will try to show that neither of these extremes is desirable, and both are unhealthy. My message will be: You *can* control your emotions without imprisoning them, and they *can* be your friends and allies.

We easily misunderstand the role of the emotions. For some, unpleasant emotions are devastating, while others are so afraid of their emotions that they are inhibited in their inability to feel. They hardly know how to really live because life is too full of painful feelings.

If you are a Christian believer, the problem is further aggravated because you can easily fall into the trap of believing that your emotions are not compatible with your life of faith. You never allow yourself to be depressed, because you believe this is unchristian. You become totally immobilized by your anger, because you don't know what is the right and Christian thing to do.

You are not alone in this confusion. There are many Christians who feel the same way. It is my purpose in this book to help you to turn your emotions to your advantage.

To some extent this book may sound like just another self-help book, and I admit that it may appear that way on the surface. However, what I have to say can hardly be construed as self-help.

The most frustrating aspect of most self-help books is that their central message is, "It is entirely up to you." Up to a point this is true, but one important ingredient is missing as far as the Christian believer is concerned. It is the availability of powerful, life-changing therapeutic resources from outside the self. If we depended only and entirely on our inner resources, we would be hopelessly lost. We truly are, in God's sight. The Scriptures are clear in telling us that the way of life in Christ is designed for our benefit, and we miss the central thrust of it all if we do not recognize and put into operation the life- and mind-changing resources that are provided. Our part is only one of cooperation—plainly and simply!

> Therefore, my brothers, I implore you by God's mercy to offer your very selves to him: a living sacrifice, dedicated and fit for his acceptance. . . . Adapt yourselves no longer to the pattern of this present world, but let your minds be remade and your whole nature thus transformed . . . (Romans 12:1, 2 NEB).

Feelings are a part of life. We cannot escape them. We can, though, easily misunderstand them. In the first two chapters, therefore, I try to make sense out of our feelings. Need they be so painful? Do they have to be self-destructive? Can they not be turned to creative use and be made to work for us, thus enhancing our lives? I believe they can, and I attempt to show what we must do to achieve this.

Chapter 3 is extremely important, and the ideas developed there are continued as a thread throughout the remainder of the book. You can control your feelings if you learn how to control your stream of thought. What you believe, assume, expect, or perceive has important ramifications for how and what you feel. Therefore, the key to unlocking the mystery of your emotions lies in understanding these thought processes.

Chapters 4 through 9 deal with the specific emotional problems that I have encountered most frequently in my practice as a psychotherapist. Chapter 10 is about joy, because not all the emotions are painful. The final chapter attempts to integrate it all by making a plea for reality in our personhood. We can only be *real* when we are authentic.

If you are a Christian, I have a special message for you. My bias throughout this book is obvious—and I make no apologies for it. Briefly stated, it is that the Christian gospel contains the essential ingredients for emotional healthiness. Resources are provided which I believe can help you make your emotions work *for* rather than *against* you. And it is because many Christians do not know how to do this that I have felt the need to write this book.

You can use this book in a number of ways:

• Its main use is as a personal study guide. Read it carefully and thoughtfully and put into practice my suggestions, and I know you will not be disappointed. I have used these techniques with scores of clients and groups and am confident that they work.

• You can use it as a study guide for small groups or with just a few friends in a home study group. Take time to discuss the contents and develop a system of accountability with each other to help you follow through on your endeavors.

• Adult Bible classes will find the book helpful as a source of discussion material, as each of the chapters can be coupled with portions of Scripture to give the contents a biblical emphasis. Additional readings, including appropriate scriptural lessons, are suggested at the end of each chapter.

• Psychologists, counselors, and pastors may find the book to be helpful bibliotherapy for their clients. It can be used to guide clients through their emotions and provide a basis for the professional therapy.

In closing, let me sound two warnings:

1. If you can get no help from this book—or if in the reading of it you realize that your problem is a serious one—I encourage you to seek professional help without delay. Life is too short and too precious for you to waste it being imprisoned by your emotions. If you don't know where to go, consult your minister or medical doctor.

2. Don't rigidly follow the specific details of this book or become deadlocked over some minor detail you don't agree with. Pay

attention mainly to the general principles and tailor your actions to your specific situation.

I have been helped along my personal journey to emotional freedom by many colleagues and friends, too numerous to mention. To the Reverend Bernard Johanson, spiritual mentor over many years, I owe a debt of gratitude for spiritual insights. To my wife especially I owe a debt of gratitude for many personal insights and for the healing love she has constantly showered upon me. A healthy marriage is the most therapeutic experience I know!

To my many clients, past and present, I owe a special debt of gratitude. You have trusted me with your minds and souls, and this has meant more to me than you can imagine. I have tried hard to conceal the identity of those I cite in the examples given in this book—and I am sure that there is no way you will be able to recognize yourselves, so don't try. I love you all too much to be guilty of callousness with what you have entrusted to me.

1

What Have You Done with Your Emotions?

As I pen these words I have just come from spending a therapy session with a client. For more than half an hour she has cried pitifully, the first time she has done this in more than twenty years. I had struggled to get her to this point for more than six weeks. She had come many times to the brink of letting her tears flow, but as her eyes began to fill she would fearfully retreat and force them to dry. Now she had had a breakthrough and was experiencing deep emotion again. At the end she said to me: "You have no idea how good it is to feel like a real person again." A real person? What a strange way to describe such an emotional episode.

Her forty-five years of life had been free of hardship. Her parents were good people and had given her most of the material things she needed in life. But somehow she had never learned how to experience her emotions freely. From her earliest years she had believed that feelings should never be shown, and the best way not to show them was not to feel them. Her emotions had to be kept imprisoned. Skillfully, she had taught herself how to hold down every hurt, every resentment, even her feelings of love, until she came to believe that she was incapable of ever experiencing any really deep feelings again. As a consequence, she had become incapable of forming any intimate relationships. Even her husband was kept at a safe emotional distance.

The therapeutic experience was both liberating and enlightening to her. She had found a way out of her emotional prison and discovered that she was not a real person because she did not have "freedom to feel."

Fortunately, not everyone has this serious a problem with feelings. Some may experience a different problem—their feelings come too often and too powerfully. They may be so shaken up whenever their emotions overtake them that they have come to despise every feeling

1

in their bodies, seeing only pain and potential destructiveness in their emotions.

The Two Extremes of Emotional Experience

We see, therefore, that there are two extremes of emotional experience. Both of these extremes can produce an attitude toward emotion that is damaging. In both cases you believe that emotions are destructive, but in the first you learn how to avoid all feelings by convincing yourself they don't exist at all and must therefore be denied or ignored. In the other extreme you just surrender to your emotions and put up no resistance whatsoever. In both extremes you miss a most important point: These are the building blocks of happiness and enjoyment. To avoid feeling is to avoid life! To feel too much is to destroy life.

How do we strike a healthy balance? That is what this book is all about. In it I want to help you come to terms with your emotions. You may not be at either extreme, but I want you to come to the place where you will be "free to feel" and have a sense of still being in control of your feelings. Feelings are to be used to enhance life, not destroy it. Unpleasant feelings can be avoided, if you so choose, without denying them; and the necessary skill for doing this is not difficult to develop. If you are a Christian believer, I want you to come to realize that you have powerful resources at your disposal for developing a healthy mind and an emotionally balanced life. You can have victory over yourself if you will utilize these resources.

The Problem of Emotion for the Christian

Many, if not most, Christians experience great conflict over their emotions. They find it very difficult to reconcile their experience of extreme feelings with their spirituality. This is, of course, all part of the larger problem that will be with us all the days of our lives. But how does one bring together the emotional side of one's being with the spiritual side? Are they at war with each other? Do my emotions have to disturb my spiritual well-being? Are there some emotions which are sinful because of the harm they cause me? These are some of the questions which plague the Christian clients I see, and they are all related to a much deeper question: "How can I be fully human, yet fully spiritual?"

I do not believe God has called us to be superhumans. One of the biggest mistakes we can make is to be misled into thinking that if we are Christian believers, we should never allow our emotions to get the better of us. It is wrong to think that we should always be in complete control of every feeling. This idea leads to inauthenticity— a sort of phoniness which ruins our witness and destroys our effectiveness in helping others. It also sets us up for developing mental and emotional problems.

I once knew a woman missionary who was one of the most controlled and disciplined persons I had ever met. Nothing could ruffle her. She was always calm, never angry, and seemed to be able to handle all the big blows that life could deal her without getting upset. On the surface she gave the impression that she was a saint, but there was something about her that made people afraid of her. Was she too perfect? Perhaps, but it was a "perfection" that hinted at inauthenticity. She couldn't really be trusted.

While she was admired by most of those who knew her and with whom she worked, her witness tended to produce guilt in others. It made them feel hopelessly inadequate in comparison with her. When her friends and acquaintances reflected on how they felt and then compared their reactions to hers, they felt hopeless failures. Rather than be attracted to her, they wanted to avoid her. She showed up their flaws! They never shared with her how they felt, nor could they ever go to her for counsel. She was too perfect. What a sad situation!

Then one day she came to me for help. "Please don't tell anyone I have been to see you," was her opening remark, as she began to tell about how troubled she was by her emotions and how she had to work so hard at keeping her feelings under control. She dared not display her feelings for fear that she would be perceived to be a "poor witness" for her Lord. I assessed her to be on the verge of a serious breakdown. Yet to the very last, she was determined not to let anyone else see her vulnerabilities. Unfortunately, this determination, to a large extent, was responsible for her problem. She was in emotional trouble precisely because she was preventing herself from giving free expression to her feelings.

As I worked with her in psychotherapy, one of the strategies I used was to move her toward being more "authentic" and honest about herself. I encouraged her to share her emotional struggles with others. As a result, she found that she could better control them. The effect on her ministry was dramatic. She was now being perceived as more human, and her struggles and other experiences became sources of insight and encouragement to others. They modeled healthy spiritual disciplines, and she taught others how to deal with their emotional struggles more effectively.

I repeat: we are not superhumans. We do not have to be dominated and disturbed by our emotions. We also need not be so afraid that we avoid them. Emotions must be woven into our spiritual lives in such a way that they produce a harmonious and complementary pattern of wholeness. Our emotions are not in conflict with our spirituality. Emotions themselves are not sinful. They do not have to disturb our spiritual well-being but can be used to complement and enhance it.

Common Mistakes Christians Make in Their Emotions

In describing the woman missionary in the previous section I tried to show that her mistake was clinging to the belief that, to be an effective witness for Christ, she had to deny and conceal her emotions. She feared that if others saw her emotional vulnerabilities, she would be discredited. By so doing she had robbed herself of all freedom to experience her feelings (known as "denial"). Consequently, she had brought herself almost to the brink of a complete emotional breakdown.

I have observed this tendency in myself. It is a common mistake made by many Christians. They skillfully teach themselves how to deny their feelings. It is a tendency also true of people in general in our culture. We discourage the display of emotions. From our earliest years we are taught (by well-meaning parents) that it is bad to be "emotional" and that feelings must never be displayed. If it only stopped there it would not be so bad, but we take it further. Not only do we conceal our feelings from others but we learn how to conceal them from ourselves as well.

Let me illustrate this point by asking you to conduct a little experiment. The next time you are with someone, stop the conversation and ask the other person to describe to you how he or she is feeling. They will stammer and stutter and probably tell you what they are *thinking*, not what they are feeling. People confuse thoughts with feelings: "I feel that I should return that dress I bought"; or "I feel that my wife is mad at me because I stayed out late." Here, "I feel" really means "I think." Recognizing and labeling feelings is very difficult for most people.

Better still, stop yourself periodically and see whether you can describe to yourself how *you* are *feeling*. It will be just as difficult. Why? We have been trained in the art of denial and the avoidance of our true feelings. We simply don't want to face our inner world where our feelings reside.

This problem can become further aggravated when you become a Christian. You move into a community of believers who, generally speaking, tend to resist the expression of real feelings. Partly it is because people are afraid of true intimacy; partly it's because this is how we all perpetuate the denial of feelings; and mainly it's because all people fear being seen as a failure. "What will they think? What will they say?" These questions haunt us. Somehow to honestly display or merely describe how we feel is threatening to our esteem and our perceived respect from others. So we intensify the "protection" of our feelings and the building of facades ("false faces") so that we will be liked and accepted.

Take, for example, the problem of anger. I recall a church meeting I once attended in which some controversial issue was being discussed. One dear brother, a respected deacon, who had served the church faithfully for many years, became angry. His face was flushed, and his lips were tight. He spoke in a loud voice and everyone became restless and felt uneasy. This was a church meeting and angry feelings were never allowed. When the deacon was asked afterward, "Were you angry?" he replied, "Never! I don't get angry that easily. I just wanted to tell them where they were going wrong!" I remember overhearing this conversation and thinking to myself, *This dear brother is killing himself with his anger—and he doesn't know it. And the reason he doesn't know it is that the church he loves so dearly and serves so faithfully won't allow him to be honest about his feelings.*

We do ourselves much harm when we cannot recognize and admit our feelings at the time they occur. This leads to emotional dishonesty and is self-destructive, not only from a spiritual and psychological point of view, but from a physical one as well.

The *first* step toward psychological and physical health is emotional honesty, the ability to recognize and own up to your feelings. The *second* step is to allow yourself more freedom in the expression of your feelings, with the goal of becoming more "real" emotionally. Only then can you become the master of your emotions and not be a slave to them. Only then can you stop imposing the most demanding and unrealistic expectations on your emotional state and find the freedom to be your true self.

Another common mistake many make, which is equally as destructive as denying and avoiding feelings, is to "give in" to your emotions in a defeatist way. "There is nothing I can do about feelings." "When that feeling comes over me, I just go away and hide." "I'm useless to everybody." These are our reactions when emotions control us rather than when we control them. And if we believe that there is nothing we can do to control our feelings, our emotional instability is aggravated and even perpetuated. Such a defeatist attitude weakens our attitude and impairs our control with time.

One important reason why such a defeatist attitude is a problem is that sufferers do not see the important connection between their feelings and their thoughts. While feelings are not thoughts, feelings are on many occasions the consequence of certain thoughts. Bad feelings can, therefore, be perpetuated by what we think and say to ourselves. I will be stressing this point many times throughout this book and will devote a chapter to discussing it in fuller detail. For now, I merely want to stress this truth: feelings are often (if not always) the result of a series of thoughts and self-statements. We can avoid prolonging our bad feelings or create good ones, by controlling what we think. Many unpleasant emotional states can be reversed by carefully examining the content of our thoughts, challenging their validity, and changing their content.

While all feelings create some physiological reaction in our glands, heartbeat, breathing, and so forth, these physiological reactions, which are an integral part of a given feeling, are also triggered by our *thoughts*. This emphasis, which stresses the relation between our thoughts (cognitions) and our emotions (affect), has recently been receiving renewed interest in psychotherapy circles. Since it is proving to be very effective in dealing with emotional problems, it is becoming the most common form of therapy. Thoughts underlie all our feelings. They may be rational thoughts or they may be irrational. But as we will see, they are the keys to understanding and controlling our thoughts. This approach is quite consistent with much New Testament teaching, where heavy emphasis is placed on the control of the mind and a great emphasis is placed on the role of thoughts, attitudes, and faith in determining our well-being. Unpleasant emotions *can* be controlled to a far greater extent than most people care to acknowledge. This "control" is not the same as avoiding all feelings. Rather, it is the effective freeing of oneself to be *more* feeling. When you are not afraid of them, emotions can be welcomed, turned to your advantage, and used to enhance your life. The key to this emotional freedom and honesty lies in learning how to deal with your thoughts.

There is yet another common mistake that we can make regarding our emotions. If you believe you are entirely responsible for everything you feel, you are not only in error but may be setting yourself up for emotional turmoil. Up to a point, it may be true that we are solely responsible for what we feel. It is possible, however, that we occasionally experience an emotional state we have neither caused nor perpetuated.

Emotions, especially the unpleasant ones, can also be caused by disturbed body functioning. Glands can become diseased and can oversecrete, or undersecrete, their powerful hormones. Parts of the autonomic nervous system can become overreactive or underreactive.

These disruptions in your body's functioning are hardly your fault, unless you deliberately cause their dysfunction by neglect or overuse.

Particularly troublesome in this regard is the thyroid gland. When it is dysfunctional it produces major emotional instability, and mood swings to either extreme can occur quite suddenly. A high percentage of women clients I see in individual psychotherapy have some problem with their thyroid gland at some time or other, and have received treatment for this disorder. Now I am not suggesting that all their psychological problems can be traced back to dysfunctional endocrine glands, but I am suggesting that hormonal problems can aggravate our bad emotional state quite significantly. The frequency with which these two problems are associated is more than coincidence and highlights how important our glands are in influencing our emotions. If you are experiencing mood swings or emotional discomfort regularly, and there is no apparent reason for this, I would recommend that you have a thorough medical examination. In fact, everyone experiencing repeated painful emotional experiences should have such an examination. It is just possible that you might be suffering from some physical disorder of which you are not aware.

Common Misunderstandings about the Nature of Emotions

Despite our general psychological sophistication (nearly everyone has taken a course in psychology either in high school or college—or so they tell me) many people hold on to a number of erroneous beliefs about the nature of emotion. These beliefs can be the cause of emotional problems themselves. I would like to comment on the four most common of these erroneous beliefs:

1. *"If I give in to my emotions, I will lose control of myself."* This is a very common belief. The underlying fear here is that "losing control" of an emotion is what causes insanity. Somehow, severe emotional distress is equated with an inability to exercise any control over a feeling. This is just not true. Serious psychological disturbances are much more complex than this, unfortunately. If anything, quite the reverse is true. Severe mental disorders are more likely to be caused by overcontrolling feelings than by undercontrolling them. If you don't allow yourself to feel, you could be setting yourself up for a major emotional problem later.

2. *"I must never let my emotions get the better of me; if I do I will be sinning."* Devout Christians often equate emotional states, such as depression or anger, with sin. Emotions themselves are not sinful. It's what you do with them that has the potential for becoming sin.

Feelings or emotions are neither good nor bad in themselves. Sometimes they serve as important signals warning us of impending danger (such as guilt or fear). Sometimes they are intended to bring healing (as with some forms of depression and grief). We need to pay attention to these signals or healing opportunities. If we train ourselves to avoid or ignore them altogether, we may be missing an important aspect of our spirituality. We may even be robbing ourselves of that which is uniquely ours as human beings, the highest of all God's creatures. God has given us the ability to feel, and it is the ability to integrate these feelings into our experience and life in Christ that separates us from the rest of the animal world. Emotions can bring us a better understanding of ourselves. Thus they enable us to live, more intelligently and completely, the lives God intended us to live.

3. *"As a Christian I should be free from emotional extremes. I should be calm at all times, never too high nor too low."* What a ridiculous idea! Fortunately some Christian groups have thrown this idea to the wind and have broken out of emotional overcontrol—at least with respect to joy and positive feelings. But they still struggle to understand how the negative emotions fit into their spiritual experience. This belief suppresses the extremes of human emotion. When our experience calls for an appropriate and intense feeling we find that we lack the ability to feel pain appropriately. We can't love when we should love, cry when we should cry, or be joyful when God opens a bit of heaven to us! We become stunted, cold, distant—overcontrolled and "blah" people. A woman came to me after a recent lecture I had given to a local church and told me that every time she heard someone praying a beautiful prayer, she wanted to cry. She asked me what she should do about her problem. I was taken aback and obviously showed it. I asked her if she knew what her real problem was. She quickly realized from the tone of my voice that she was overly concerned about "what others would think" of her. I told her that it was perfectly normal to cry when you feel moved. I do so all the time. She could allow herself to cry as often as she wanted to. I saw the relief in her eyes that this advice brought to her. They welled up with tears. "Feel free to feel" is the essence of emotional healthiness.

4. *"Prayer alone can take away emotions that are out of control."* I know many are sincere when they believe this. God does answer prayer. There are many who feel that the only thing they can do whenever they are sad, depressed, hurt, upset, or angry is pray. And so they should! But when I ask them what it is they pray about, I invariably find that they are praying about "that other person" or

whatever it is that is *causing* their feeling. "Please, God, take John away!" or "Give me what I want," is the usual prayer. Seldom do they focus on themselves and the feelings they are experiencing at that moment. They won't admit what it is they are feeling so their prayer is not focused on the real problem. Our feelings are often the only source of true information about what is troubling us. We need to pray for more feelings, not less.

The joy of emotional freedom. Humans are complex emotional organisms. Our emotions (and the way we cope with them) is probably what separates us most widely from the rest of creation. Animals cannot feel as we do. Their responses are "conditioned responses," not expressions of free, intelligent, and emoting creatures. Your dog may wag its tail as a sign of love to you, but the love you are capable of showing to others, as well as to the dog, far surpasses anything your pet has to offer. Your feelings do not have to be conditioned responses to what others have done for you. You have the capacity to be totally unconditional—to give love without regard to any reward.

Through your emotions, you have the potential for deriving the greatest pleasure and joy which life has to offer. Emotions provide the excitement and thrill of living that no other aspect of your being can provide. Take away your capacity to feel (and this has been done in times past in certain forms of brain surgery) and life suddenly loses its luster. No feelings—no life. Such a person no longer feels the thrill of excitement, the flush of embarrassment, the sobering of a disappointment, or the happiness and joy of some new discovery or adventure. Feelings, both pleasant and unpleasant, give your life its sparkle and they should therefore be embraced, understood, and taken charge of in such a way that they are used to enhance life.

On the other hand, emotions also have the ability to cause great misery. Lose control of an unpleasant emotion, such as depression, and you will soon lose any reason for wanting to live. Every suicide is probably caused by the sufferer not wanting to feel any more pain. This reality should not cause us to want to avoid our emotions. It should motivate us rather to turn them to our good. God has given us the capacity for utilizing our complex emotional systems for the greatest benefit, and it should be a force that draws us nearer to Him and not, as so often happens, away from Him.

To help us become emotionally free so that we are able to experience emotions in a healthy, positive, constructive way, God has provided us with many resources. As we proceed we will identify and apply these resources. With God's help, we can make our lives more abundantly joyful. My goal throughout this book will be to show you how this is possible.

Summary

There are two extremes of emotional experience, and both can produce an attitude toward emotion that is destructive and self-defeating. Either we allow our emotions to overwhelm us, and therefore come to fear them as if they were the "enemy within," or we overcontrol them and rob ourselves of the many rich experiences they can bring. It requires effort to strike a balance between these two extremes to know how to be "free" to feel our feelings. Emotions can be made to work for you and bring the happiness and enjoyment God intended them to bring. This does not come naturally. It takes hard work!

The problem of emotion is even more complicated for Christians who must contend with integrating the emotional side of their beings with their spiritual side. There are many mistakes that we make as Christians in dealing with feelings, including encouraging each other to deny our feelings, succumbing to emotions in a defeatist way, and believing that we are totally responsible for everything we feel. A healthy attitude toward emotions, with the recognition that they are God-given and intended to enhance our lives, can free us to experience them in a healthy way.

Additional Reading

1. *Emotional Common Sense: How to Avoid Self-Destructiveness,* Rolland S. Parker (New York: Harper & Row).
2. *Healing for Damaged Emotions,* David A. Seamands (Wheaton, Illinois: Victor Books).
3. *Feeling Good about Your Feelings,* Barry Applewhite (Wheaton, Illinois: Victor Books).
4. Romans 12.

2

Our Confusing Emotions

Psychologists probably know less about emotion than about any other broad topic in the field of psychology. This is because emotions are very complex. They cannot be studied in the laboratory as easily as other reactions. Poets probably do a better job of describing them. Indicative of the great complexity of the emotions is the considerable theorizing that has taken place about them over the years. We know more about learning, perception, development, and even the nature of personality, than we do about emotion. Descartes, who lived from 1596 to 1650, might just as well have written his *Passions of the Soul* in our day, for in it he states: "There is nothing in which the defective nature of the sciences which we have received from the ancients appears more clearly than in what they have written on the passions."

While our emotions may be as much of a mystery to ourselves as they are to the scientific psychological community, I don't mean to imply that we cannot control them. We can avoid or reduce many unpleasant and unwanted emotions and learn how to induce positive ones. Acquiring this ability can radically change a personality and transform a life from being unbearable in its pain to becoming a satisfying and deeply meaningful experience. To do this we must first come to grips with the confusing nature of our emotions and have a clear understanding of the many factors that produce our feelings.

We are complex emotional organisms, and many factors contribute to our emotional states. We are also as distinctively different in the area of the emotions as we are in personalities or our fingerprints. Each of us is unique, and we produce our particular emotional patterns quite differently. If you are a male, you will not respond to the world in quite the same way as you would if you were a female. Your age, your physical health, your personality, and a host of other factors will all have a major influence on how you experience your emotions.

Have you ever wondered whether the feeling of depression you experience is *exactly* the same as that experienced by some other person? How can you ever know? Unfortunately, you can't enter into another's experience and find out. All you have to equate your feeling with another's are the outward signs of the depression. You recognize enough similarity to what you are experiencing for you to be able to identify and label them as the same. No two people, however, ever experience *exactly* the same emotion. Each of us is unique, and each feeling we experience is *our own*.

The Complexity of Emotions

How many emotions are there? This interesting question has always fascinated philosophers, poets, and psychologists. It cannot be answered as easily as you might suppose. One reason is that the terms used to describe emotion are often vague. Finding good technical terms for the various emotions has been extremely difficult, and this task has been magnified by the tendency for psychological traditions to perpetuate their biases.

Another reason it has been difficult to establish a sound classification for the emotions is that they are themselves extremely complex. Take anger, for example. It is a whole variety of emotional reactions, not just one single type of experience. To fully describe a particular person's anger you will have to take into account his age, the situation, preceding factors, and much more. To say that a child is angry is not the same as saying that an adult is angry. Animals certainly cannot be "angry" in the same way as we can, but they do show aggression. If there are that many aspects to anger, how is it possible to describe them completely by the single term, *anger?*

William James, one of psychology's giants, tackled the problem of emotion as early as 1884 when he published an article entitled "What is Emotion?" He later proposed the idea that there were basically two *levels* of emotion. At the first level we have the "coarse" or fundamental type of emotion, of which there are four: (1) grief; (2) fear; (3) rage; and (4) love. The second is a "fine" or subtle level of emotion which is derived from combinations of these four fundamental types.

While this theory would not receive acceptance in all psychological circles, it does have value in emphasizing a number of important points which can help us understand how our emotions work. Let me draw attention to just three:

1. If James's theory is correct, there is basically a very limited set of fundamental emotions from which we derive our many feelings. These variations on the primary emotional theme may be caused by

situational factors, and this gives us the impression that we experience many more emotions than we really do.

2. It would be wrong to believe that there is no overlap between our emotions. There are no clear boundaries between one feeling and another. It is possible, for example, to be feeling both anger and depression at the same time and for these not to be separate feelings, but an amalgam of one. This could have important implications for how you deal with your emotions, as there is in this instance only one and not two feelings to be dealt with.

3. Emotions are not simply "in your head." It is easy in this age, when everything is psychologized, to believe that emotions are purely "psychological." Quite the contrary! We should always remember that our emotions involve a complex interaction between psychological and physiological factors and that we cannot separate the one from the other. True, it is often your thoughts, attitudes, and beliefs that trigger your emotional state, but the emotion does not come into existence until some aspect of your physiology has been activated. Once the thought or idea has been removed, therefore, you must not expect your emotion to go away immediately. Depending on the severity and type of emotion, it may take a little while for your physiology to return to normal. This is often overlooked in cases of anger and depression.

Misconceptions about the Nature of Emotion

We are plagued by many misconceptions about the nature of emotion. We perpetuate these misconceptions without thinking about their full meanings and the implications they have for our mental health. These misunderstandings tend to create more problems than the emotions themselves, because they have such a powerful influence on our expectations and behavior.

Again, take anger as an example. One common misconception, unfortunately also held by many psychologists, is that anger can be "stored up": If it is not released periodically, it will cause us some mental harm. This idea treats anger as an entity, an energy of some sort, which can be accumulated like water in a tank. It leads us to believe that we can do nothing to stop the process and that once the anger tank has been filled it *must* be drained off. I will discuss this misconception in more detail later in this book, but let me at this stage pose this question: If it is possible for anger to be stored in this way, why do we not also store love, joy, envy, fear, and so on? The answer is that emotions simply do not accumulate— they do not exist as single quantities or entities. They are "states." They are the final product of complex interactions between our minds and our bodies. The variety of these combinations is infinite, and this is probably why poets have done a better job of describing the emotions than scientifically trained psychologists. Perhaps poets know how to put feelings into their situational and personality contexts. They are not hung up on science and thus are better able to capture and describe the true essence of our emotions.

Other misconceptions about the nature of emotion commonly held by Christians are:

1. A Christian should never be subject to extremes of emotional reaction.
2. It is sin that causes emotional disorders.
3. Our parents are to blame for all our emotional hang-ups.

These ideas are patently ridiculous and yet are considered true by many. Consequently, they cause unnecessary guilt and suffering. Being a Christian does not stop us from being human and from being subject to those emotions which are normal responses to life's experiences. True Christians have resources available to deal with many of life's problems, but they should not expect to be completely devoid of feeling. Emotions are God-given and inherently good for us. Something has gone wrong when we allow them to become destructive.

Feelings vs. Emotions

Up to this point I have used the terms *feelings* and *emotions* interchangeably. To be technically correct, we should distinguish between them, as they do have slightly different meanings. *Feelings* are basically a part of emotion. They are the part of emotion that breaks through into our awareness. A feeling is the sensation or bodily state that accompanies the experience of the emotion. What we feel depends on our interest and attention at the moment of experiencing the emotion. If we are not attending to our emotion, we may not *feel* anything, but the emotion is still there. On the other hand, *emotion* refers to the deeper, underlying state that stirs or agitates us, whether or not we are aware of it as feeling. The term *emotion,* therefore, refers to the state of our being. Feeling is how we experience that state. For practical purposes we might as well use both terms interchangeably.

It is unfortunate that we have also come to use the term *feel* to describe activities other than emotion. We "feel" with our hands. We even "feel" with our intellect, as when we say, "I feel that you have as much right to sit by the window as he does." It is not surprising to find that this multiple use of the word *feel* has contaminated our understanding of how to experience feelings. We often shortchange ourselves because we don't really understand the difference between the true feeling of an emotion and the many other things we "feel." This may cause some people, especially men, to engage in intellectualizing or rationalization and yet think they are "feeling."

Emotional Chaining

One important point to remember about your emotions is that they are not always an end in themselves. Just as the first echo causes many others, one emotion can be the cause of another. The sound of an echo keeps bouncing backward and forward between mountain surfaces until it finally dies by losing energy. Similarly, you can react to an emotion within yourself, then develop another emotion, and this then creates a third, and so on. Fortunately, the process finally weakens and eventually dies for lack of energy. Sometimes, however, it does not weaken. There can easily be an escalation in the severity of an emotion. It goes from bad, to worse, to terrible. I call this "emotional chaining." It is an extremely important principle and can help you understand your emotions and develop a healthy way for controlling them.

As an example of how emotional chaining can take place, let us suppose that you have become depressed over the loss of your job. Such a loss generally creates feelings of frustration, since the loss represents a major obstacle to the achievement of your life's goals. Being frustrated, you also become extremely angry and may seek some way to express your anger. You could write a nasty letter to your immediate supervisor or blame someone else for your job loss. As soon as you realize that you have become angry, you may well trigger some depression. The depression then intensifies because you believe that you are not in control of yourself. More depressions may mean more anger—and the cycle can repeat itself over and over again until your depression reaches serious proportions. This is the process of "chaining," where one emotion creates another and keeps the process going for a while. If you pause for a moment, you will easily recall examples from your own life of how one emotion has created another, in this chaining pattern. Perhaps a disappointment of some expectation caused you to become hateful toward the one who disappointed you. Embarrassment can give rise to self-hate and self-rejection. Jealousy can cause the most intense anxiety feelings. Emotions, therefore, are often linked together in a chain. When you rattle the first link, you activate the whole chain.

I knew one person who was very prone to this chaining pattern. It nearly caused her to lose her life. In a fit of anger one day she walked out of her home with the intention of moving in with a friend on the other side of the city. In her fantasy she was expecting her husband to follow her, find her, and then plead with her to come back home after declaring his error and begging for her forgiveness. No sooner had she left home, slamming the door behind herself, than a deep sense of embarrassment came over her for her uncontrollable anger. This sense of loss (which was really a loss of self-esteem) triggered a severe depression reaction. She felt that should could not face herself—let alone her family—for doing this, so she decided that the only way out was to take her own life with an overdose of sleeping pills. Fortunately, the attempt failed, and nothing more than a sore stomach was the consequence.

We are able to chain from one emotion to another because we have the capacity to reflect upon and evaluate our emotions. We tend to label them as "good" or "bad." This causes us to react with further emotions, depending on what value we place on the first. We fear and want to avoid certain emotions. Certainly not proud of ourselves for being angry or jealous, we want to feel that we are in complete control at all times. We don't enjoy embarrassment or making mistakes, so when we experience these feelings we react to them with fear or disgust and thus create a further emotion. This new emotion is often more intense and disastrous than the original.

What can we do about this chaining? The *first* step is to come to know yourself well enough so that you can recognize when you are chaining your emotions. Your past experiences can tell you whether you are prone to this. Examine the expectations you have of yourself and others and see whether they are too idealistic and demanding. Do you, for example, expect never to fail? This is unrealistic and irrational. Whatever else you might believe about yourself, you need to remember that you are only human and therefore must make room for occasional failures. Try to develop an attitude which tolerates failures as a necessary part of learning. Examine your fears of emotion: Where do they come from? Do you need to be so afraid of them? By facing these fears openly and honestly, can you reduce their power to create unpleasant reactions? Once you stop creating new emotions out of existing ones, your battle is half over. You can then focus your attention on the original emotion and take steps to deal with it. Where do emotions come from? Do you need to be so afraid of them? By facing these fears openly and honestly, you can reduce their power to create unpleasant reactions to your emotions. Once you have developed some ability to stop creating new emotions out of existing ones, your battle is half over, since you are then free to focus your attention on the original emotion and take the steps necessary to deal with it.

Psychotherapy and Emotion

From my discussion so far, you can see why it is so difficult for people to "get in touch with" their emotions. It is possible for an emotion to exist for a long time without our ever identifying and acknowledging it. We have a remarkable ability to avoid our emotions. Consequently, it is possible to be totally ignorant of what is going on inside.

This is not true for people of other cultures. Some cultures teach their members to express their emotions more directly than we do. These people are not afraid to show their feelings. They may shout a lot and engage in a variety of histrionics, but they show what they feel, when they feel it, with great freedom. They are not afraid to be labeled as emotional. The remarkable consequence of this cultural style is that there appears to be a lower incidence of neurotic disorders. Noise and broken china may be a problem, but neurosis is quite rare! Psychiatrists and psychologists are jokingly described as finding it hard to make a living in these cultures.

This raises a very important but vexing question. Given the emotional restrictiveness of our culture, what are we supposed to do with our feelings? We cannot suddenly change our cultural patterns, and the advice we receive from popular books and magazine articles only increases our confusion. We are told to "release" our emotions. This idea is grossly misleading. It implies that something is dammed up inside which must be drained away. Since emotions are experiences which involve every part of one's being, how can we "release" them? Another misleading expression is that we are told to "look at" our emotions. There is nothing to look at. We can only "feel" them. Perhaps what is meant is that we should "reflect" on what we are feeling. Emotions are dispersed throughout our being like salt dissolved in a glass of water. How can we possibly look at the salt? Emotions can be felt, experienced, and reflected upon, but never "seen." What, then, are we to do with them?

We may get some help here if we take a moment to examine what psychotherapists do when they work with a client's emotions. While therapeutic styles differ greatly, there are common features in all psychotherapy. From psychoanalysts to behaviorists, what is common?

1. *Psychotherapists explore the events that precede an emotional experience.* To be able to identify all the factors that precede an

emotional experience is extremely important in coming to understand an emotion. Unfortunately, the one experiencing the emotion may frequently be so taken up with how he or she is feeling that he or she fails to fully realize what it was that caused the feeling. Often the real cause is not the one that is presented by the client. Therefore, the psychotherapist helps to identify the *real* cause of the emotion.

A husband may suddenly find himself depressed. At first he does not know why he is depressed, but then his wife comes to him with the monthly bills and reminds him that they have not yet caught up with their Christmas spending. He immediately launches into an attack on her, accusing her of being a "loose" spender and having no consideration for how hard he works. Implied in this attack is his belief that his wife is the cause of his depression. In actuality he has only just found a convenient excuse to blame for his depression. The real cause may lie in some recent event in his work that he was not confronting realistically. Of course, it is possible for multiple causes to lie behind an emotion, and we cannot always precisely determine the exact factor. But the explanation of preceding events is very important in freeing oneself from a painful emotional state. Sometimes it is sufficient merely to eliminate the more obvious cause and thus relieve our friends, spouses, and children of responsibility for how we feel.

2. *Psychotherapists increase the person's awareness of emotion.* Emotions have the ability to exist and yet elude our awareness and attention. In psychotherapy, we help individuals to become more aware of emotion by focusing attention on what they are feeling from time to time. Often we will stop and ask a client, "What are you feeling at this moment?" By so doing, we train the client to monitor his or her feelings. But a person who cannot understand the cause of such feelings may only be further confused by being made aware of them. The purpose of increasing awareness of feeling is to force the person to identify and face the underlying cause of the feeling. A client may avoid recognizing or wanting to talk about the real problem. By increasing awareness of feelings, and even allowing him or her to become angry or cry, the therapist is moving the client toward a place of courage and willingness to face the real problem.

3. *Psychotherapists clarify the nature of a person's emotion.* As therapists, we encourage clients to "taste" rather than "look" at emotion, to *feel* rather than *think.* Often this involves helping clients to build a "feeling vocabulary," so that they can more accurately describe what they are experiencing. Our language is notably deficient when it comes to expressing feelings. This is one of the reasons why we find it so satisfying to use verbal obscenities. Swear words,

because they often do not have any precise definition, can take on many different meanings. Combined with their shock value, they can serve to provide a release for our feelings which is quite unique.

It is not my aim to advocate swearing as a healthy outlet for expressing feelings. I am only trying to point out that, by helping clients to *accurately* label and describe how and what they are feeling, we provide both understanding of underlying problems and clarification of the corrective steps that need to be taken to resolve their feelings. This is quite different from the idea of "releasing" your emotions by, for example, allowing yourself to cry or become angry. This is called "ventilation" and under some conditions it can be helpful. However, raving and ranting over and over again may never solve any of your problems. You may, in fact, find yourself becoming a more and more angry person in the process, or tending to cry much more easily. Our goal is more than experiencing emotions. It is their *clarification* and this comes from accurately labeling them so that you can better understand what *causes* them.

4. *Psychotherapists facilitate the experience of emotion.* Spending one's life overcontrolling and suppressing emotion can use up a lot of energy. A person who lives this way is very prone to develop a neurotic lifestyle. Often this overcontrol generalizes to all the emotions, so that if you cannot allow yourself to feel angry, you also won't allow yourself to love or be loved. It is difficult to train oneself in controlling only one emotion while letting all the other emotions have their freedom. Thus, as therapists, we may take "tasting" a step further and encourage someone to experience an emotion very deeply. A client is only able to do this when he has a great deal of trust and confidence in the therapist.

I recently had a fifty-year-old woman as a client whose husband had been killed in an automobile accident five years before. When I first saw her she was complaining of insomnia, headaches, and general tension. As we explored her problem, it became obvious that she had never recovered from her husband's death. Life had come to a standstill for her, primarily because she had not completed her grieving over the loss. My therapy focused on helping her experience her grief as deeply as possible. This was painful for both of us, but gradually, out of this deep experiencing of her grief, she began to pull her life together again.

5. *Psychotherapists encourage a more open expression of appropriate emotion.* An emotionally free or healthy person is someone who knows what causes his or her emotions. This person can attend to, identify, and describe them and is free to experience all feelings to an appropriate degree. If our culture is at fault it is for training us

to "overcontrol" our emotions. Obviously, then, we need to move ourselves to a freer experience and expression of them.

Unfortunately for many, the only safe place for this is in the trusting, confidential, and professional nature of a therapeutic relationship. Where else can you be yourself so completely? Where else can you say what you think without it backfiring? It is a sad thought to me that we who profess to have received unconditional grace from our Creator should find it so hard to show the same grace to our fellow creatures in giving them total acceptance. Love is something we talk a lot about in Christian circles, but we have a long way to go in demonstrating it. Our attitude to emotional experiences and the taboos we place on their expression are major factors in preventing us from fully experiencing love in our Christian communities.

Fortunately, there is one other place where you can be yourself totally and completely and have the freedom to express your emotions unreservedly. It is the place of prayer! No doubt many of you have found this to be the most therapeutic of all life's experiences. I never cease to marvel at what I know can happen there!

Our Many Selves

Another mistake you can make in trying to understand your emotions is to divide yourself into "life compartments," and then see yourself as being made up of these separate compartments. You may see yourself as having an intellectual compartment, a physical compartment, a reasoning compartment, and so on. Nowhere is this idea more misleading than in the area of your emotions. Just as there are many aspects to your total being, there are also many aspects to your emotions, and you should constantly remind yourself that you do not function as a dismembered machine but as a totally integrated being. It is artificial to separate your mind from your body, your emotions from your thoughts, or your actions from your intentions. As the Gestalt psychologists would say, "The whole is more than the sum of its parts," and this applies as much to your emotions as it does to anything else. There can only be value in examining the parts of your being if you don't make the mistake of seeing these parts in isolation from one another. We must always remember to put Humpty Dumpty together again, even though there is value in studying the parts.

One common way in which we compartmentalize ourselves is to separate the psychological aspects of our beings from the physiological. As Christian believers we would probably want to make this a three-part compartment and add our spiritual dimension also. This compartmentalization extends even to the health care services, where we have established separate professions for taking care of the psychological, the physiological, and the spiritual needs of humankind. While some effort has been made to restore the whole by emphasizing the interactive aspect of these compartments (for example, through the psychosomatic-medicine emphasis) the average layperson still tends to think of him or herself in terms of separate aspects of being.

Why is it important not to do this? Mainly because people do not make allowance for the other parts. They believe they can have feelings without glands. Physiological factors can play an important role in influencing emotional conditions—and vice versa. We could also say that spiritual conditions can influence both physiological and psychological states. I certainly know that when I am fatigued, both my psychological *and* spiritual well-being are affected. To be emotionally healthy we must be sensitive to these interactive factors.

I have, for example, had a number of clients who have complained that they frequently experience periods of depression. In examining their lifestyles, habits, and so on, I have found that they are invariably overworked, eat poorly, don't know how to relax, and are caught up in a constant round of pleasing everybody they encounter. They complain of always feeling fatigued and never take time for recreation. The interesting thing is that seldom do they realize that there is a connection between their fatigue and their depression. After providing them with some help in rearranging their priorities, teaching them how to relax effectively and making sure they eat well-balanced meals, their depression diminishes drastically. Of course, not all depression goes away this easily, but it is important to realize that your physiology is an essential part of your emotional being. If you disturb or abuse your physiology, you will pay for it in the coinage of emotional pain. It does not take a genius to see where the problem must first be tackled.

The Danger of Ignoring Obvious Physiological Factors in Emotion

Some physiological disturbances, however, are more permanent in their effects and much more difficult to correct. For example, some diseases or brain states are not that easy to predict, nor do we know how they cause emotional disturbances. There is one form of depression, for example, that is described as "endogenous," meaning that it comes from within the body. It is not related to any obvious environmental factors, as no identifiable precipitating event can be located. There is strong evidence to support the idea that it is caused by a biochemical disturbance in the body often triggered by stress. Those who suffer from this disorder do so for many years without seeking professional help. When it is offered they refuse to take it, simply because they don't understand that the real cause is in their physiological make-up, more than their psychological.

What happens if we do not allow for these physiological factors? We tend to look in the wrong places for the reasons for our unpleasant emotional states. We look around in our environment for factors to blame, and if our husbands or wives, our children, our employers, our friends, or our pets and even God are conveniently available, we may place the blame on them. In blaming them, we inappropriately set the stage for further disturbances. Those we blame may feel unjustly accused and may engage in a counterattack to defend themselves. This is how emotional wars are started.

An example of this occurred with a married couple I once worked with. From the time they were first married they had caused each other considerable emotional pain, despite the fact that they claimed to love each other dearly. The husband was depression prone (of the endogenous variety). Every time he felt "down" (averaging about once every two or three weeks), he would blame his wife for his depression. Since she was only human, he did not have great difficulty in finding something that he could blame. She would become upset at his accusations and would defensively pull away from him and refuse to talk. This caused further depression, and he would then intensify his attacks on her. After many days of misery, the depression would finally go away, they would make up—only to have the cycle repeat itself again after a few weeks. There was enough variety to the cycle so that the pattern eluded their attention. The saddest part of all was that they claimed to be Christians, and the turmoil of their marriage had caused much havoc to their spiritual lives. They were on the point of giving that up also.

When they finally came for help about their problem, I referred the husband for appropriate medication to stabilize his endogenous depression and taught him how to deal more directly with his depression proneness. He quickly learned how to stop blaming his environment for his depression, and their marriage began to mend.

In another case, the wife was clearly at fault. She experienced periods of emotional disturbance that resulted in uncontrolled episodes of confusion. She put the blame for this on her husband until their first child was born and then blamed both the husband and the child. Even when she was separated from her spouse (as occurred when she had to be left at home alone due to the nature of his work), she continued to blame him. At first the husband believed she was right and tried everything to placate her. Eventually he became exasperated, realized that he was not entirely responsible for her feelings, and demanded that they seek professional help. Unfortunately the wife was not very responsive to therapy and refused to undergo an appropriate evaluation for the cause of her confusion states. She was fixed in her belief that the husband was to blame. Their marriage eventually broke up. Such an unhappy outcome is most unfortunate, especially since I was convinced that her problem was physical in nature and could easily have been corrected by treatment.

Summary

Our emotions are extremely complex. As a result they are confusing both to ourselves and to the scientific community. While we seem, as human beings, to be capable of a wide variety of emotional experiences, they probably can all be traced back to only a relatively few basic emotions.

Misconceptions about the nature of emotion abound, and they tend to create more problems than the emotions themselves. It is important, therefore, that we have a clear understanding of what causes and what perpetuates our emotions.

Chaining of emotions—where one emotion gives rise to a second as a reaction to it—makes it difficult to identify the original problem. This keeps us in a perpetual state of confusion. To avoid doing this requires that we stop continually labeling what we are feeling as "good" or "bad." If you are feeling something, go ahead and feel it. Give yourself permission to do this and you will not react with further anger, depression, or self-condemnation.

What happens in psychotherapy, as we learn how to become freer and more accepting of emotions (particularly the unpleasant ones), is a good model of what we should be doing in our daily lives. We need to train ourselves to explore the events that *precede* an emotional experience, increase our awareness of the present emotion, clarifying what the emotion is and then be more open to experiencing feelings.

Additional Reading

1. *Our Many Selves,* Elizabeth O'Connor (New York: Harper & Row).
2. *The Kink and I: A Psychiatrist's Guide to Untwisted Living,* James D. Mallory and Stanley Baldwin (Wheaton, Illinois: Victor Books).

3. *Spirituality and Human Emotion,* Robert C. Roberts (Grand Rapids, Michigan: Wm. B. Eerdmans Publishing Co.).
4. *The Experience of Psychotherapy: What It's Like for Client and Therapist,* William H. Fitts (New York: Van Nos Reinhold).
5. Romans 6.

3

How Thoughts Cause Emotions

Proponents of a form of therapy called "Rational Emotive Therapy," stress that human beings seem to have a natural tendency to think crookedly and therefore easily establish and maintain self-defeating patterns of behavior and emotion. By "crooked thinking" Dr. Albert Ellis means the tendency to think irrationally or to hold on to the most ridiculous beliefs, despite evidence to the contrary. This tendency to think irrationally, he contends, is a major cause for what we experience as "neurosis." More importantly for our purpose, he would contend that it is a major factor in causing many of the emotional upsets we experience.

I don't agree with everything that Rational Emotive Therapy says, but I do agree on some points at least. The purpose of this chapter is to show that even as Christian believers, we are not immune to this tendency to "think crookedly" and believe the most ridiculous ideas. We can have as much crooked thinking in our Christian belief systems as we have in any other area of our lives. This is not an error of the basic truths of the gospel. In my opinion they are healthy and health producing. But we are only human and most of us have derived our beliefs from secondhand sources and have consequently assimilated all the distortions of those who have ever influenced us.

The Confusion in Psychology

We have recently come through a period of great confusion in some schools of psychology about how to handle our emotions. Believe me, psychology hasn't quite got its act together! There has been far too much preoccupation with feelings themselves and not enough emphasis placed on the importance of what *causes* feelings.

While there is therapeutic value in expressing and experiencing one's emotions (and this is certainly an essential part of being emotionally healthy), the actual feeling or emotion is only the end of a chain of events. If one is to learn how to avoid an unpleasant emotion, it is necessary to look at the thought events that precede that emotion. This is what the cognitive theories of psychology emphasize. As a group, cognitive therapists are growing in number, and they stress that emotionally disturbed persons are not victims of concealed forces beyond their awareness and over which they have no control. Emotions are neither mysterious nor impossible to control. They can be explored and understood in the context of one's learning history and current patterns of thinking.

This approach has great appeal to me, not only because it provides a powerful and effective therapeutic tool, but because I can see in it important concepts for integrating theology and psychology. The gospel places great emphasis on beliefs and their power to shape our lives. Of course, it is not merely the nature of belief per se that is important, but also the truthfulness of and the content of the belief. When one believes a set of truths as powerful as those contained in the Christian gospel, one is at least shaping many powerful beliefs about human nature, love, forgiveness, and hope which must have an effect on our emotions. When we exercise faith, we are exercising belief. Faith in Christ, though, is more than mere belief in Him. It is an act of surrender to Him and His saving work.

As a Man Thinketh

James Allen wrote a wonderful little book many years ago called, *As a Man Thinketh*. In this book he says (using Proverbs 23:7 as a foundation): "A man is literally what he thinks, his character being the complete sum of all his thoughts."

I would take this idea further and reword what Allen says as follows: "People feel what they think. Their emotions are the complete sum of all their thoughts." I am sure that James Allen would agree with me if he were alive today, based on what he has to say in the rest of his book. Born in 1864, he died in 1912, at the young age of 48, but in his little book he was able to describe much of what would become our modern approach to cognitive therapeutic psychology. Listen to what he has to say:

> The body is the servant of the mind. It obeys the operations of the mind, whether they be deliberately chosen or automatically expressed. At the bidding of unlawful thoughts the body sinks rapidly into disease and decay: at the command of glad and beautiful thoughts, it becomes clothed with youthfulness and beauty.

If we substitute *irrational* for "unlawful," *emotion* for "body," and *misery* and *unhappiness* for "disease and decay," no modern-day cognitive therapist could have said it better. The thoughts of our minds determine whether we will be happy or miserable, successful or a failure, composed or angry, relaxed or tense. Except in those rare disorders (psychosis, brain damage, or obvious physiological disturbance), we must accept responsibility for all that we think and feel. While biological and environmental factors may interact to influence our emotions we retain the capacity to intervene between the environmental input (what is happening to us) and the emotional output (what we feel) in nearly all instances. If I did not believe this I would not do psychotherapy.

Potentially, at least, we have an enormous amount of control over what we feel and do. The real problem is that we lack the motivation and understanding to intervene. Most times when psychotherapy fails it is because the client is unwilling to make any effort to change. The advantages of changing do not pay a bigger dividend than the present self-defeating behavior or emotion. We could all change if we wanted to.

The Importance of Thoughts in Producing Emotions

Thoughts are important in influencing our emotions primarily because they give meaning to the events that happen to us. Thoughts, in turn, are influenced by our beliefs, attitudes, expectations, assumptions, and perceptions. Before discussing these in more detail let me outline the chain of events that lead up to an unpleasant emotion. The most common understanding of what happens is as follows:

EVENT ——————— (produces) ——————→ EMOTION

An example would be: A woman's husband criticizes her in front of her friends (Event) and this causes her to become so angry that she cannot talk the rest of the evening (Emotion). This woman believes that the criticism was the direct cause of the anger. In Rational Emotive Therapy (a form of cognitive therapy), the *cause* of an emotion is called the "activating" event (A) and the final emotion is the "consequence" (C). Thus A causes or leads to C. What is frequently overlooked is that there is always an intervening variable—some set of "beliefs" (B).

The essence of the cognitive approach is to emphasize that between the A and the C there is an intervening B. My "belief system" determines what I feel when something happens to me. Thus, A can only cause C through B, hence the A-B-C approach to understanding many emotions. What happens is as follows:

$$\text{EVENT} \longrightarrow \text{MEANING} \longrightarrow \text{EMOTION}$$
$$\text{(Activator)} \qquad \text{(Belief System)} \qquad \text{(Consequence)}$$

It is the intermediate belief system that gives meaning to the event, and the emotion is a consequence of this meaning and *not* of the event.

For example, the woman whose husband criticizes her in front of her friends becomes angry because her intervening belief system gives some meaning to the criticism. It mediates between the event and the consequence and is the *primary* cause of the consequence. The "meaning" may relate to him not loving her or to the fear of being embarrassed in front of her friends. True, it may all happen in a split second of time, and the woman may not have to think consciously about the event. But the "meaning" is still operational and the consequence is still the product of her belief system. She may interpret the event as rejection; she may fear that her friends will believe what the husband is saying; she may not want to face up to her own inadequacies; or she may simply fear that this criticism will ultimately lead to rejection. These are all aspects of *beliefs*. They must be understood before the angry feeling can be understood.

While this can all happen very rapidly, in the "blink of an eye" so to speak, there may be times when we have ample opportunity to think about something that has happened to us. The emotional consequence may not arise immediately. It may follow our mulling over the event and engaging in a lot of self-talk: "What did she mean when she said that?" "What is he hiding from me when he tells me that he will be late?" We muse and search our belief systems through the medium of thought, and then create feelings that match our beliefs. Unfortunately, most times these are unpleasant emotions.

The influence of our beliefs on our emotions has long been understood. As far back as Marcus Aurelius (A.D. 121–180) we can trace ideas that speak to this issue. In *The Meditations* he writes, "If you are pained by an external thing it is not this thing that disturbs you but your judgment about it." In other words, it is not people's actions that affect us, but our reflection upon and reaction to their actions.

Emotions Can Be Changed

What is important about all this is that our emotional reactions are *not* permanent parts of our personality. Rather, these emerge out of how we see ourselves, others, and God. Our beliefs, ideas, and attitudes determine our emotional reactions in pretty much the same way as a rudder determines the direction a boat will sail. True, the wind (our environment) and the ocean currents (our biology) may have something to say about the overall direction, but these forces can be transformed into other powers that determine direction and negate the influences of the wind and current to our advantage. All it takes is a little effort on our part and it soon becomes a natural process. If you are criticized, you can turn that criticism to your advantage by using the same thoughts that would have devastated you. By remaining objective and rational, you can examine the criticism to see where it is justified and then take appropriate steps to rectify those defects. You can actually grow through such experiences. Those elements of the criticism that are not true can be discarded. Let me again quote James Allen on this point:

> A noble and Godlike character is not a thing of favor or chance, but is the NATURAL result of CONTINUED EFFORT in right thinking . . . he is the maker of his character, the molder of his life, and the builder of his destiny, if he will watch, control, and alter his thoughts, tracing their effects upon himself, upon others, and upon his life and circumstances.

Believe me, such wisdom would take scores of therapy hours to learn.

How Are Thoughts Formed?

In our waking moments we are bombarded by a stream of thoughts. These thoughts are influenced by what is going on around us as well as what is happening *inside* us. Thoughts have their origin in both conscious and unconscious activity. If you are driving on the freeway, having just come from an important business meeting without eating lunch, your thoughts are likely to be switching from the events of the meeting, to the cars and people on the freeway, to lunch, and then back again. This "stream" comes on continuously.

You may also be anticipating other activities for the afternoon. After a while your thoughts may focus entirely on what is yet to happen. The stream of thought is with you all the time. Occasionally you may pause to reflect on the content of your thoughts and if I were to measure the physiological reactions of your body such as your heart rate, respiration or sweat gland activity, I would be able to see a very direct picture of this stream of thought. It has a continuous influence on your body. It may speed up your heart, then slow it down again. It may cool your hands, then warm them again. Constantly you are being prepared for action then calmed.

All this activity is under the influence of your thoughts. Your ability to handle stress is very much dependent on the "reactivity" of your physiological system to this stream of thought. Some of us have very reactive bodies, and we pay for this in headaches, ulcers, and high blood pressure.

Overall, our thoughts are determined and greatly influenced by our fixed beliefs, attitudes, expectations, assumptions, and perceptions. Either singly or in combination, these will determine the meanings we attach to events. In a split second after something has happened to us, the reaction will set in. It doesn't need a lot of conscious processing—it is preprogrammed. Because they are so important, let us examine each in turn and see how they operate to affect your thoughts and hence your emotions. From a better understanding of them we can learn more effective ways to control them.

- *Beliefs:*

These reflect the acceptance of something as true. For example, in theology a belief is the firm persuasion of the truths of a doctrine. Our beliefs are formed and shaped by a number of factors. One powerful influence is experience. We believe that airplanes can fly because we have seen and experienced their flying. I doubt if anything can shake this belief. We also believe that men have walked on the moon, although we have only seen pictures to prove this. The day it was announced that the United States had placed a man on the moon, I was talking to an old African lady in South Africa. She was illiterate and very cautious. She told me that she only believed what she could see with her own eyes. I asked if she knew that a man had just stepped from a moon rocket onto the moon's surface. She turned her head and laughed. She thought I was joking. How could anyone believe such a thing! Her experience could not allow her to accept this as truth.

"Did you see this man?" she asked me.

"No," I replied, "I only heard it announced on the radio." I don't mind confessing that I felt a little sheepish at her challenge. But if at that moment some action was called for which depended on that belief, I would have responded to it with my very life. I knew it was true, even if I had not seen the man myself. We had different beliefs, formed by our different experiences.

But not all our beliefs are formed by experience. Some beliefs are deeply ingrained in our minds even though we don't have a shred of evidence to support them: Beliefs about the world, ourselves, the future, and the past. Some beliefs are concrete while others are very abstract. I may believe that 1) when my car's tires are worn to a certain level, I run a high risk of having an accident in wet weather; or 2) unless I am outstandingly competent and never fail in any project I undertake, I will not be accepted by my friends. The first belief is "rational," since there is evidence to support it. The second is an example of what Albert Ellis calls an "irrational belief" as there is not a shred of evidence to support the idea.

I realize that these terms are used rather loosely, but, generally speaking, they are useful labels for two types of belief. They help to contrast those beliefs that can be empirically demonstrated (rational) with those that have no substantiation whatsoever (irrational). Whenever we invoke absolute ideas such as "I've got to!" "I must" or "I ought," we are invariably invoking irrational ideas. These irrational beliefs give rise to irrational thoughts which are then followed by illogical thinking. When this occurs with deeply personal matters, the emotional consequences can be disastrous.

To illustrate this point: being short, bald, or having a long nose is not really a problem in and of itself. One may have to stretch, wear a hat, or mind your own business, but life can go on quite normally with these contingencies. In contrast, it is clearly most irrational to believe that because you have one of these supposed defects you are not acceptable to others. There is no law or principle that says one must be tall, full of hair, and have a Roman nose to be accepted by others. If your belief about such attributes has become distorted and their importance exaggerated, so that your life is full of fear of rejection, then you are allowing an irrational set of beliefs to control your life.

It is not uncommon for otherwise healthy people to be controlled by such irrational ideas. Most of us carry in our heads these and other ideas and are resistant to their extinction. Many of these distorted beliefs are acquired in childhood and they don't grow up with us. We become adult but our beliefs remain childish. We then perpetuate them throughout our lives by failing to challenge or dispose of them. We only become aware of these irrational beliefs after we have suffered from their consequences. Seldom can we recognize them before they get us into emotional trouble.

Some irrational ideas we hold to are quite universal in character. Many have been identified and found to be quite common in emotionally disturbed people. They are probably present to some extent in all of us. If we hold to any of the following beliefs we are clearly crossing the line from rational to irrational thinking.

- I must be loved and liked by everyone.
- I must be loved at all times, without exception.
- I must be perfectly competent in all that I do.
- I must never fail.
- I have no control over my own happiness.
- Everything bad that happens to me is catastrophic.
- Everyone must treat me fairly.
- I must experience pleasure rather than pain in my life.

The irrational flavor of these ideas will become obvious as you think about them. They are based on *absolutes* (no exceptions, blacks and whites rather than grays) and set up expectations way beyond what can be reasonably expected from human beings. These and similar irrational ideas, to the extent that they are believed and held unconsciously, can lead to many negative emotions. It has been demonstrated over and over again (and I have experienced this working with many clients) that when a person—

- deliberately confronts and examines the ridiculous nature of these ideas . . .
- stops expecting them to be true . . .
- stops condemning himself or herself for being human and unable to meet everyone else's expectations . . .
- realizes at the deepest level of his or her being that God accepts us in Christ *just as we are* . . .
- stops judging him or herself and others for being human (only God has the right to judge) and . . .
- utilizes the resources of the gospel to help overcome all of this . . .

such a person can practically eliminate most of the more serious and unwanted, unpleasant emotions. Does such a claim sound too bold? Perhaps. If it does, I apologize for making it sound that way. But the positive nature of this statement is intended to make a point: we are not as out of control as we think we are when it comes to dealing with our emotions.

- *Attitudes:*

These are also important in the formation of thoughts and in influencing our emotions. By "attitude" I mean the disposition or tendency to respond in a particular way to people or objects. Attitudes can have their origin in our beliefs, or they can be completely independent of them (or at least appear to be so).

Some attitudes have the ability to create in us those "split-second" response emotions which follow quickly on the heels of some event. Therefore, they have tremendous power to disturb us. We have learned from past experience how to respond to a given action without any apparent thinking at all. An attitude is thus a "preprogrammed" response to a given action.

For example, a prejudice is a biased attitude usually learned through imitation and involving emotional rejection and hostility. We all have such prejudiced attitudes and biases, but few of us are aware of them. If you are a typical middle-aged person staying in a holiday-resort hotel and a group of young people move into rooms on the same floor, it is highly possible that you will immediately react to their presence with anger (without even thinking). Your sleep will be disturbed just knowing they are there. This will probably spoil the rest of your holiday. What has happened? Something triggered your prejudice about young people. Your attitude toward them was then prearranged. You do not know when you first see them whether they are well-behaved or rowdy, and you probably did not even stop to think about it. Your feelings were triggered automatically by your prejudiced attitudes. The same would be true if you had been the one to intrude on a group of young people. Their attitudes toward you would have been determined by their prejudices.

Changing an attitude is a very complex task. In this short review on how our thinking influences our emotions I couldn't possibly give you any comprehensive guidelines. What I can say is that you can go a long way toward reducing your prejudices and ensuring healthy attitudes by—

- openly *admitting* that you are subject to many prejudices (since we are all safe in admitting this) . . .
- being *on guard* against negative attitudes . . .
- *stopping yourself* as soon as you become aware of the attitude or prejudice that is triggering your emotion and . . .
- *challenging* it with all your mental ability and forcing yourself to see the other side of the issue and identify the reasons for your reaction.

Let me illustrate this with the example I gave you earlier. Let us suppose you are the middle-aged person enjoying your vacation at a seaside resort. You notice that a group of young people has just arrived and occupied rooms close to yours. Initially becoming annoyed and even angry, you say to yourself, "Now I will never get any sleep! I've paid all this money only to get a bunch of rowdy kids in my hair." You realize you are angry, so you stop yourself, admit that your attitude to these young people is prejudiced from past experience, and then prepare yourself to be open to some new insight.

"Need I get angry?" you can ask yourself. "My anger is not going to remove them. How do I know that they will be rowdy? I have no evidence for this. Perhaps I am only envious of their youth and jealous of the ability to have fun so easily and freely. If they disturb my sleep, I will ask them nicely to be considerate of my needs. In the meantime, if I am nice to them instead of being angry, I will achieve two things: 1. I will recapture some of my lost youth and get some vicarious satisfaction from being around some fun; and 2. I will win them over as friends, so that if I have to ask them to be considerate, they will be only too happy to oblige 'such nice people.'"

Perhaps at this point you will have noticed that your emotional *pain* has become emotional *pleasure*. Is this difficult to achieve? Only if you do not want to take the time to watch, control, and alter your attitudes—or if you prefer emotional pain to emotional pleasure. Such self-control is not only healthy, but I believe it is a spiritual response to such circumstances.

Notice one very important point about this technique. What we say to ourselves (through our *self-talk*) plays a major role in influencing our emotions before and after they have been triggered. Your initial anger reaction could easily have been intensified if you had said to yourself: "I should never have come to this place. Everything always works against me. Nobody respects me any more. . . ." I think you recognize a famous comedian here (Rodney Dangerfield).

If we can only control our self-talk and begin to think and talk more rationally and objectively, we can do a turnabout in our emotions. This takes some practice and the investment of a little effort, but its rewards are peacefulness and joy. Unfortunately, it seems to be so much easier for us to "go with the negative" thoughts and self-talk, almost as if we prefer to be miserable rather than happy. As self-talk is so important to emotional happiness, I will devote a special section to it toward the end of this chapter.

- *Expectations:*

"He always comes home late from work, goes straight to his favorite chair, opens the newspaper, and gets lost in his reading. He never comes and kisses me first, and I do not like his behavior."

"Why," I ask my client who by now has tears streaming down her face, "do you continue to make yourself miserable by expecting your husband to be different? He has never come home from work and kissed you as his first act, so what makes you think he is going to be any different the next time?"

This kind of conversation occurs regularly with clients. Someone always expects someone else to be doing or saying something. If the complaint is not about a spouse, it concerns children, bosses, and even pets! We set ourselves up for depression, for anger, for rejection, and for defeat by convincing ourselves that we have a right to expect something. That "something" can be love, respect, consideration, and much more. We build up a hope that something will happen at a certain time (with very little real cause to expect it), and when it doesn't happen we experience an emotional disappointment. This is the problem of "expectations." Unfortunately, some of them are quite reasonable and we deserve them. Often, however, they are not.

When my wife and I first came to California, we looked for some property to purchase and I found a piece of land that I fell in love with. It had a magnificent view and there was a "For Sale" sign on it. As we looked the land over my imagination ran wild. I imagined myself, as owner, building a lovely home, subdividing some of the land to pay for the home, and generally living a contented life. I telephoned the realtor whose name was on the board, and he thought I could purchase the land for a reasonable price. My expectations ran even higher. My hopes filled out like a hot-air balloon and soared away on the winds of my imagination. The blow came a week later. "I'm sorry, Dr. Hart, but the owner tells me that he does not want to sell the land anymore!" The realtor's message was most disappointing. I had failed to keep my expectations in check so the loss I experienced was as devastating as if I had actually purchased the land and had someone steal it from me. Even though I had never owned it, it was still a great loss for me.

There are many instances in life where we set our expectations unreasonably high. Because they are not met, we experience a letdown and the most unpleasant emotional reaction. We anticipate some gift or we build up our hopes for some dream to come true, and when it doesn't turn out as we anticipated we are deeply disappointed.

While some expectations are reasonable, many have no basis in reality whatsoever. If we expect to be loved (or at least liked) by everyone, we *will* be disappointed. This is an unreasonable expectation. Only some people can like us. Inevitably others will not. This is a fact of life! If we expect never to fail or make a mistake, we will also be disappointed. Some failures are inevitable and mistakes will happen whether we like it or not.

These may appear to be extreme examples, but subtle variations of these expectations are part of everyone's make-up. They center around spouse, children, parents, jobs, friends, and churches. They are the source of many disappointments.

We can deal effectively with our expectations by injecting a lot of "reality testing" into them. When you next find yourself setting up an expectation, ask yourself: "What law or principle says that such and such must happen? Would it not be better if I did not set myself up for such an expectation? Then, if it does happen I could receive it as a surprise."

I like to teach my clients the art of "bonus building." I say to them: "If you expect something to happen and it does not, you will be disappointed. If you do not expect it and it happens, you will have received a bonus." In other words, it is far better to receive a happy surprise than to be disappointed. There are many areas of life in which we can apply the principle of "bonus building."

The most important effect of this change in attitude is that we do not experience the extreme of emotional reactions that usually go along with disappointment. These emotions often disturb our social milieu and cause arguments between spouses, children, church members, and many others. The wife who is disappointed because she is not first kissed when her husband comes home from work may become angry and pout the rest of the evening. Her reaction will anger the husband who does not understand how important a symbol of his love the kiss is, and he eventually gets angry also. This will affect the next time he comes home. It's a vicious circle that someone must break. Very soon an angry stalemate sets in. If the wife's expectation is not set up in the first place, the emotional conflict could be avoided and the social atmosphere improved. She may never get her kiss, but at least there can be peace! The real issue can then be discussed in a calm, anger-free environment. The issue stands a better chance of being resolved when there is a calm atmosphere than when anger and counter-anger prevail.

- *Assumptions:*

These are things we take for granted. In this context, they refer to the tendencies we have to take for granted what people say or do for us. A husband may make a dinner reservation and *assume* that his wife remembers he told her that he was going to take her to dinner on their wedding anniversary. When his wife acts surprised he reacts with anger. "Didn't I tell you I would do this six months ago?" This tendency to make all sorts of assumptions is the cause of many marital conflicts.

Perhaps you assume that a friend will know where and at what time to pick you up for some engagement. If he fails to fulfill your assumptions, you react with anger.

It seems that it is a very common human trait to make assumptions about many things. These assumptions are mostly caused by faulty communication or just plain laziness in failing to check out the correctness of our information. As with so many other human weaknesses, we seldom take active steps to correct such behavior.

- *Perceptions:*

Early in our marriage my wife came home one day and said, "I saw the strangest thing today. I was coming out of the supermarket and a car turned the corner in front of me. It only had three wheels."

"You mean," I replied, "it was a three-wheeler?"

"No, it was a regular car, but it was riding on only three wheels."

Well, you can imagine how I responded to such a ludicrous idea. "Come on now," I said, "no ordinary car can stand on only three wheels. You know that. Why do you think I use a jack to change a tire? It's not possible for a regular car to drive on three wheels." I was emphatic and thought I had settled the argument.

But she was adamant: "The car only had three wheels, one wheel was missing. It was traveling in front of me. In fact, it turned the corner just as I came out of the supermarket." She was emphatic—and a stalemate followed.

Very soon it became a full-blown argument. For many months afterward it was the source of much disagreement between us. I thought, *Why could she not understand the laws of nature?* She probably thought, *Why does he not believe me when I tell him what I saw?*

Well, what eventually resolved the matter for me was the realization that things are not always what they seem. Facts are not as important as perception. "Seeing" is, after all, always just perceiving, and "perception" is always subject to some distortion.

Unfortunately, the trouble is that we believe what we perceive. We believe what we *think* we see. What is actually true may be quite different.

Now I have never finally settled this difference of opinion. I happen to believe that what my wife saw was only a perception. Perhaps due to a shadow cast by the car, its angle, and some other factors, she only perceived three of the car's four wheels. For her, though, the perception was *reality*. I was failing to recognize the accuracy of her perception. She was asking me to simply accept the truthfulness of her statement, not engage in a scientific debate!

In the realm of our ideas and thoughts, we are always subject to some distortion of our perceptions. I am not referring so much to what we see as I am to our thoughts, ideas, and feelings. It is absolutely essential that we realize three important facts about the way we psychologically perceive things:

1. It is not the facts of a situation that determine how we react, but our *perception* of these facts.

2. The way we perceive something may be quite different from what actually happened.

3. We must always give others credit for the way they perceive things and not insist that the only way things are is how we perceive them. I now believe my wife saw a car with only three wheels!

Arguments between friends and couples often arise over differences in the way they perceive things. I am almost tempted to say that it is the most important single cause of interpersonal friction. Misperceptions or differences in perception cause confused communications and create issues where no issues ought to exist.

If your wife says to you that she thinks you are too friendly with your best friend's wife, what is important is that she *perceives* it this way. If you insist, according to the facts, that she is wrong, become upset at the fact that she can even make such an accusation, and demand that she retract it with an apology, you are in trouble! You are making the fundamental mistake of not recognizing that what is important for her is *not* that you have no ulterior motive, but that from her perspective what you are doing is causing her to perceive the situation as she does. Give her credit for her perception and you will begin to heal the relationship. Ask yourself whether you are to blame for some behavior that causes her to see things the way she does. This will open the way to better communication and move you to be more understanding and tolerant.

Which Comes First—Feelings or Thoughts?

No doubt my emphasis here on how thoughts cause feelings may lead some of you to ask: "Which comes first? Is it not possible that it is the feeling or emotion that *causes* the thought rather than vice versa?" Yes, this is possible. But it appears to be much less frequently the case than the other way round. The best way to understand what happens is to realize that thoughts and feelings are a two-way street.

If a thought occurs first and then creates a feeling, very soon this feeling influences thoughts. If a feeling arises first, it generates a set of thoughts—and these thoughts then interact with the feeling. Often you cannot separate the thought from the feeling. Much psychology has focused on and emphasized the *feelings-producing-thoughts* sequence. In recent years this emphasis has begun to move to a greater appreciation of how thoughts produce feelings.

In the final analysis, both approaches are important, and neither should be neglected. I have chosen to place greater emphasis on how thoughts work to influence feelings because of the relative neglect of this approach. It is also a lot easier to control thoughts than it is to control feelings.

Thought processes are not only important in creating feelings but also serve to *maintain* the feelings. Emotions receive their sustenance from the continuous things we say to ourselves. It appears to be extremely difficult to sustain an emotional upset without bolstering it by repeated ideas and thoughts. If someone insults you—and you become angry—you can only keep being angry if you *continue* to say to yourself, "How could he [she] say such a horrible thing to me?" If you stop doing this and challenge the accuracy of how you interpret the insult, you can recover from the effects of the insult much more quickly.

The Importance of Self-Talk

As I have indicated, most of our thoughts take the form of conversations we have with ourselves. We call this "self-talk" and we are not always aware of our doing it. As an exercise, you may wish to observe your thoughts more closely and identify the conversations you have with yourself. Keep a notebook alongside you through the day and jot down these conversations. We cannot have thoughts without them affecting our feelings. To be aware of your self-talk will help you see issues more clearly and reduce your muddled thinking.

If you are going to learn how to reduce your disturbing emotional experiences, you will have to monitor very closely what you say to yourself. By doing so you will discover your irrational beliefs, attitudes, expectations, assumptions, and perceptions. In fact, self-talk can serve very effectively as a "window onto your thoughts."

You can take the monitoring of your thoughts a step further and actively begin to interject healthier ideas into your stream of thought. For example, instead of saying to yourself, "It makes me angry to hear her criticize my daughter like that," you could say, "It is most unfortunate that she finds it necessary to criticize my daughter this way. When she stops I'll have a quiet chat with her about it." Again, instead of, "It's terrible that I have to put up with such incompetence on this committee," you could say, "I'll make do with the best talent available. Perhaps we'll learn how to work together better."

These are just a few examples of how we can turn apparent and self-made reactions into positive experiences. Our natural tendency is always to look on the negative side—mainly, I suppose, because the only way we can feel good about ourselves is to find fault in others. We find it difficult to resist the need to catastrophize, and we exaggerate disaster out of all proportion. We then spend our energy dwelling on the apparent catastrophe rather than on taking steps to remedy the situation. It takes discipline and deliberate action to turn these thoughts around and say the right things to yourself.

Let me quote James Allen once more: "There is no physician like cheerful thought for dissipating ills; there is no comforter to compare with good will for dispersing the shadows of grief and sorrow. To live in thoughts of ill will, cynicism, suspicion, and envy, is to be confined in a self-made prison hole." Wise words indeed!

Summary

Do you want to be free? Do you want to be in control of your emotions and not have them control you? Do you want them to be your friend and not be afraid of them? Do you, as a Christian, want your emotions to enhance your spiritual life rather than work against it? You can only do this if you rise up and take control of your thoughts. The "stream" of your thoughts will be the most important factor in influencing how you feel. If you can keep firm control of your thoughts, you will not be subjected to extremes of emotional buffeting. If you watch, control, and alter your thoughts by patient practice and trace their effects upon you and others, you can move yourself to the place of emotional freedom. I trust that the remainder of this book will help you to do this. My prayer is that we will discover together that Solomon was right when he said, "For as a man thinketh in his heart, so is he . . ." (Proverbs 23:7 KJV).

Additional Reading

1. *As a Man Thinketh,* James Allen (Old Tappan, New Jersey: Fleming H. Revell).

2. *Fully Human, Fully Alive,* John Powell (Niles, Illinois: Argus Communications).
3. *The Wider Place,* Eugenia Price (Grand Rapids: Zondervan Publishing House).
4. *You Can Become the Person You Want to Be,* Robert H. Schuller (Old Tappan, New Jersey: Fleming H. Revell).
5. Philippians 2:1–16.

4

The Problem of Anger

Contemporary psychology has not yet found an answer to the problem of anger, although there is probably no other emotion that has caused as much confusion and disagreement among psychologists. The subject has provoked so many different ideas about how to deal with it that the average lay person must feel utterly frustrated every time he or she reads a book on the topic by a psychologist. Almost every self-help book has something to say about anger, and there is little agreement amongst the writers about the "how to." What this means is that psychologists really do not understand the problem of anger. We may know a few things about it. We know that it can elevate blood pressure; that for some reason we can actually enjoy being angry; that the capacity for anger is built into our nervous systems; and that anger probably serves some primitive, instinctual, protective purpose in helping us overcome obstacles that block the way to our survival. This is hardly enough to help us deal with our anger.

Is anger good for us? Are we better off if we allow ourselves to be angry, or should we try to control our anger? Is anger "stored up," requiring some sort of occasional release? Do we have to show that we are angry, or is it sufficient to merely acknowledge but hide it? Do we sin when we get angry?

These and many similar questions bombard our minds when we think about anger, and psychology has not yet come to any agreement on what the answers to these questions should be.

Theology does not seem to have helped us much either. I deal in therapy with many who claim to be Christians, including ministers, and they have not come to terms with their anger either. They experience much conflict over what to do with their anger and the consequent guilt often creates depression. Much sincere preaching condemns anger either directly or by inference, and Christian communities do not provide a clear understanding of the nature of anger or how to deal with it. While I do not want to give the impression that I have discovered the key to unlocking this puzzle, I do believe there are a number of important principles which can help us in this dilemma. As you explore these with me, you may find some help in your struggle against anger.

Anger and the Christian

Many well-meaning Christians find themselves caught in a struggle over their anger. On the one hand they get the message that anger is bad. They feel so "unchristian" whenever they give expression to their anger. Their communities discourage any show of anger, and this leads to a pervasive fear of making people angry and of dealing with someone who is angry. Because all angry feelings must be suppressed, group activities become difficult and often unpleasant experiences, and committee meetings mean pain and frustration.

I can recall some of my own frustrating experiences in working with church committees where no expression of anger was tolerated. Every hint of bad feelings caused a chain of reactions which could not be handled by any of the parties concerned. Relationships became reduced to superficial encounters, and everyone kept everyone else at an emotional arm's length to avoid being hurt.

On the other hand, much contemporary psychology has emphasized that anger should be freely and uncontrollably expressed. We are encouraged to lash out at everything and everybody we please. "Don't bottle it up, but let your anger out," we are encouraged on every hand. Our culture has almost come to worship those people who can be angry all the time. We admire them in therapy groups and believe they are the only put-together and free people.

One book on anger (I'm glad to see that it is no longer popular) even suggests that every person should develop a variety of rituals for releasing bottled-up anger. The impression I get in reading such advice is that life consists of a continuous struggle to find ways for blowing off steam at every opportunity. I have a sneaking suspicion that the people who practice this are miserable within themselves as well as with those with whom they live. Unfortunately, everyone else has to pay the price for the privilege that one angry person claims for him or herself.

Parents also often believe that children should be free to have temper tantrums as frequently as they like. They teach their children (if not directly, then certainly by their example) how to kick the furniture, the cat, and anything else that gets in their way, in order to ventilate their angry feelings. Unfortunately, the long-term effects of this behavior are not appreciated, especially since this can easily become a deeply entrenched lifestyle if it is encouraged.

Such individuals usually end up acting this way all their lives, making life a hell for everyone else.

The Dilemma

There is something very satisfying about giving in to your anger. No doubt you have found this out for yourself. When you let go and lash out at everything around you, it feels wonderful (if you can avoid the feeling of guilt afterward). It is far better than the utter frustration of having to bottle up your rage. But no sooner have you done this than you will be overcome by a deep sense of guilt. This is the dilemma: what should one do with anger? Believing on the one hand that anger is condemned and should therefore be suppressed, yet deriving so much relief from ventilating it, you are left feeling either extremely guilty for letting go, or more frustrated and angry from having to bottle it up.

Should anger be condemned? Is there not a difference between the emotion of anger and its expression as hostility and aggression? We are told that it is healthier to express one's anger than to suppress it. The expression of anger is indeed a healthier alternative to suppressing it. But is there an even healthier way—that of not having anger at all? Is there a constructive and creative way to deal with angry feelings without compromising one's faith and causing discomfort to others? I believe there is. A proper understanding of anger and its workings is essential to the forming of community, obeying the command to love, and building happy families. Intimate relationships such as marriage can only survive if we know how to deal with anger. Effective committee work requires a clear understanding of the dynamics of anger, and maturity in the Christian faith can only be achieved as one makes progress in mastering one's anger.

The Nature of Anger

We all know what anger feels like—but do we know what it is? One unabridged dictionary defines it as "a strong feeling of displeasure excited by a real or supposed injury: often accompanied by a desire to take vengeance or to obtain satisfaction from the offending party." The key words in this definition are *strong feeling, injury,* and *vengeance.* Anger always has these three components, and we will see that the key to dealing with anger lies in dealing with these components.

While anger may have served some function for humans in more primitive settings and may now be useful in emergency situations, modern everyday life seldom calls for legitimate anger. It is nearly always destructive in relationships and is often hazardous to our health. The prolonged experience of anger has been linked by some to problems such as high blood pressure (essential hypertension) and an increased risk for heart disease. Anger disturbs our happiness and seldom moves us toward being fulfilled persons. It disturbs marriages and often incapacitates and immobilizes us. Severe anger can even be a form of temporary insanity. The person is completely out of control and dangerous to those around. Most child- and wife-beatings take place under conditions of extreme anger, and many murders are committed in anger where there is a need to take vengeance.

Is Anger Ever Necessary?

Under what conditions is anger essential and necessary? Do we ever have to get angry—or could we get by without it?

In our modern lifestyle the need for real anger as an essential emotion *seldom* arises. We need to understand that anger is a survival emotion—a signal of threat. Occasions where we need anger for our survival may occasionally arise but they must surely be very rare.

I can think of one such occasion that occurred some years ago with a colleague of mine. This will serve to illustrate my point that anger as an essential emotion is *seldom* legitimately needed.

Waiting for his daughter one evening, my colleague was sitting with his wife and a friend in his automobile outside an apartment building. Three young men with revolvers accosted them and demanded that they hand over their money and jewelry. My colleague, a senior professor in his early eighties, was sitting in the back seat. He was utterly stunned by the actions of these young men as they began to pull the jewelry from the two women in front. One of the men held a revolver at his wife's head.

At first the robbers did not notice him in the back of the car. Finally one of the men saw him and came around to open his door and take his money. As the car door began to open, my colleague became extremely angry and overcoming all fear for himself, he kicked out with both his feet. The young man went flying. His friends panicked and fled.

Discussing the incident afterward, my colleague told me that it was anger that gave him the courage to do what he did. Anger triggered the resources he needed to perform the actions he could not have done otherwise.

Anger helps to motivate us to overcome obstacles. The display of anger protects us by frightening away assailants. In more primitive cultures and certainly in the animal world, we see clear evidence for this use of anger. In our modern lifestyle and western culture, however, we seldom need to make use of this anger. Life is far more "psychological" and less "physical" for most of us. Our obstacles are not robbers but criticism and therefore more subtle. Our enemies are less tangible and our fears mostly imagined. Of what value, then, is anger? Perhaps it is because we no longer have a legitimate role for anger to play that it has become a major problem for us and a serious disturbing factor in our relationships.

A Model for Understanding Anger

Even though anger is not altogether needed in modern life, it still arises. Our culture does not teach us how to handle anger; rather, we are trained to suppress it or give expression to it in devious ways. In order to be able to cope with anger, it is useful to have a clear understanding of how anger is created. While the model of anger I will present here is somewhat simplistic, it contains the essential elements for understanding the problem and can be used with confidence to guide you in coming to understand the nature of anger as you experience it.

Figure 1 presents this model. There are four *levels* to be considered: the origins of anger, its causes, its expressions, and its resolution. I will discuss each in turn.

1. *The Origins of Anger.* For the origins of anger we need to consider both the biological and the learned components, as both contribute to the creation of anger. Anger is one of the primary emotions present at birth. If you hold a baby down so that it cannot move, you will elicit the instinctive rage response which is necessary for survival. Specific parts of the brain have been identified as being responsible for this anger response. Whenever a particular provoking stimulus is experienced, the nervous system responsible for anger becomes activated. It is possible to activate these parts of the brain directly through electrical stimulation and thus elicit the anger response in the laboratory.

The important point for us is that the normal stimulus that activates the anger response is psychological, not physical. In other words, the ideas, thoughts, and perceptions we experience, and our interpretation of these events can trigger our anger response. These triggers are acquired primarily through learning. There is, therefore,

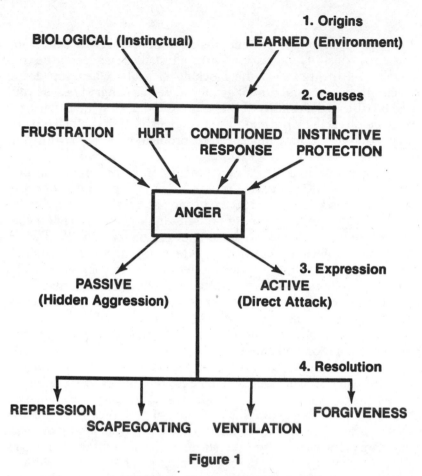

Figure 1

A Model for Understanding Anger

an important connection between what we think and experience and the in-built, biologically determined mechanism of anger. It takes no more than a thought to trigger anger. Once it is triggered it becomes a biological state. The implications of this will become clear as we proceed.

2. *The Causes of Anger.* Anger can be caused or triggered through four main mechanisms: *frustration, hurt, conditioned response,* and *instinctive protection.* The first two are probably more important from our point of view, since they are most likely to be the major cause of anger for us, given our westernized life-style.

Frustration

One of the more important theories about anger is called the "frustration-hostility-aggression" theory. It states that anger is the consequence of frustration or the blocking of goals. When you desire something strongly and cannot get it, you become angry because your need is frustrated. Primitively, this anger is intended to help you overcome the obstacle by provoking you to attack it. It doesn't take much imagination to see how this can be a problem at work or with your spouse!

Obstacles to our goals can take many forms. Anything that prevents you from obtaining what you desire has the potential for creating anger. Obstacles can be *physical* such as breaking a leg the day before you are due to play an important tennis game, or having your car break down on the way to work. They can be *social,* such as when your spouse won't agree to go to a movie with you, or when someone refuses to show you the respect you feel is due to you. We can also have *personal* obstacles: low self-esteem, feelings of inadequacy, or a history of being rejected by others as being unattractive or incompetent. These obstacles can be very subtle and difficult to identify on the one hand, or obvious and visible on the other. They all give rise to much frustration and anger.

Conflict situations can also give rise to frustration and anger. By "conflict" I mean the simultaneous arousal of two or more incompatible goals. This occurs when you are torn between two equally attractive opportunities and must choose only one. Are you going to give up a summer fishing trip to be with your family on vacation? Both are desirable. Will you stay in a marriage for the children's sake, even though you have been attracted to another partner? Will you follow the ethics of your Christian commitment and thus avoid having a "good time" on a business trip? These are illustrations of some major conflict situations. They also create anger.

Not all conflicts are as major as these, but even petty conflicts can cause just as much frustration and anger as those I have just mentioned. Will you go to play golf—or support your son at a Little League game? Will you go on working to support your husband in graduate school—or will you get on with your own studies? Life is full of these potentially anger-producing situations. They can keep you at boiling point for a long time.

How do we deal with anger that is caused by frustration? There are three important steps.

1. *Develop a more flexible personality.* Improve your ability to adapt to changing situations. Rigidity in your expectations and

responses is a sure sign of neuroticism. You can become more flexible in a number of ways. For instance, keep a careful lookout for events in your life that cause you to become angry, no matter how small they may appear to be. As soon as you realize you are angry, try to see whether you can identify the underlying frustration. Is there something you want that you can't get? Is someone blocking your way? Have you lost something or are you about to lose something?

Frustration can take many forms, and it may be necessary for you to talk over your anger with a family member or close friend in order to identify it. Pay attention to how you feel and especially to what you are saying to yourself. Remind yourself that you need to be flexible, and let go of anything you may be clinging to unnecessarily. Deliberately and consciously doing this gives you the feeling of being in control and maximizes your ability to be flexible.

You can better prepare your children for handling frustration later in their lives by teaching them that they don't need to receive everything they want immediately. Low frustration tolerance in children (and in adult life) is a common symptom of our age and is the cause of much unhappiness. We perpetuate this low tolerance for frustration in our children when we give them everything they want *immediately*. Learning how to delay gratification and postpone the fulfillment of our desires is an important step toward maturity and a healthy emotional life. We cannot always get everything we want immediately! Irrationally, though, this is what we expect. Consequently, we experience repeated frustration and anger.

2. *Learn to accept and be happy with compromises.* In the minds of some, the idea of *compromise* is not acceptable. It implies that you are lowering your standards, your ideals, or your goals, and settling for something that is second best. I don't mean it in this sense. I believe that most of us are hung up on having this "perfection." We are obsessed with wanting to be the absolutely best mothers, fathers, children, lovers, workers, or students. We abhor failure or mediocrity and try to avoid it at every opportunity. We despise ourselves every time we show any signs of imperfection.

We have great difficulty accepting the limitations of our humanness; our incompleteness. We are *not* gods! Christ came to save imperfect people (which is what it means to be a sinner), and while we remain human we will have to accept the reality of our limitations. To "compromise," in the healthy sense of this idea, is simply to accept our imperfections and be content to do the best we can. Since this frees us from fearing failure, we are often more effective in whatever we attempt.

3. *Work at knowing yourself.* What motivates you? What causes you to react the way you do? I never cease to marvel at how naive we are about ourselves, our inner motives. We know a lot about how our friends function and don't hesitate to give advice when necessary. We know little about ourselves. Nowhere is this self-ignorance more damaging than in the area of frustration and anger. If we do not know *when* we are frustrated or *what* frustrates us, we will not be able to deal with the source of our anger. Frustrated dependency needs, ego needs, love needs, security needs, and a host of other needs, can constantly keep us experiencing anger over which we have no control—simply because we don't understand ourselves and our motives.

Hurt

The next important cause of anger is *hurt.* Anger as a response to hurt arises whenever we experience physical or psychological pain. Have you ever had someone tramp on your toe? The pain you experience immediately triggers a reaction of anger and a strong desire to hurt back. Children demonstrate this to us again and again. Johnny pulls Mary's hair, and immediately Mary wants to do the same (and more) back to Johnny. When we become adults we substitute humiliation or criticism for hair-pulling. It's still the same game!

Psychological pain can produce just as strong a desire to hurt back as can physical pain. If you are criticized, do you stand there calmly and take it? Not if you are human. Even if you do not give immediate expression to your feeling of anger, in the back of your mind you are tearing the other person apart with counter-criticism and fault-finding. Most sarcasm is a subtle way of "hurting back." Since this is the most common cause of anger I will discuss it more fully in the next chapter.

Conditioned Responses

These causes for anger are learned early in life. Some don't even have to be learned—they are natural reflexes. For example, we learn how to get our way by *displaying* anger. Parents, teachers, brothers, and sisters reinforce this behavior by giving us our way whenever we display anger. We remove obstacles and manipulate our friends by displays of anger. Sometimes we show anger in more subtle ways, such as pouting, negativity, and threatening. It's all designed to do the same thing—get our way.

The temper tantrum of a child is another good example of a "conditioned" anger response. On the very first occasion of a tantrum the child may only have experienced a frustrating response to not getting what he wants. The anger outburst was embarrassing to the parent. The child notices this, then repeats the display until the parent gives in to the wishes of the child. If this is repeated a few more times, the child quickly learns (both consciously and unconsciously) that when he becomes angry and causes an embarrassing disturbance, he can get anything he desires. The temper tantrum has become established as a conditioned response.

Temper-tantrum anger is, of course, more intense than frustration-anger, and the child gives it a flare with lots of screaming to accentuate its manipulative purpose. These children later learn to substitute other forms of anger so that when they grow up they continue to utilize conditioned forms of anger to manipulate people and get their way. I call this "emotional blackmailing." It is *very* common in dysfunctional people.

As an aside, how should one deal with a temper tantrum, a child's or an adult's? Very simply: *Ignore it.* Walk away. Forget the embarrassment. *Never* give in to the demands of a tantrum—you'll regret it the rest of your life.

Instinctive Protection

I have already mentioned that anger can serve as a form of "instinctive" protection. This form of anger provides us with the motivating and energizing force to protect ourselves. It gives courage to overcome obstacles and fight off threat. Policemen and soldiers learn how to use this anger to face danger and do their duty. If kept in check, it is a healthy form of anger. However, our present lifestyle does not often call for physical means of self-protection. Ordinary life seldom demands that we use this form of anger. Our problem with anger lies clearly in the areas of frustration, hurt, and conditioned responses.

The Resolution of Anger. We resort to a number of devices for resolving the anger we experience. Not all of these are helpful or healthy. The three most common are *repression, scapegoating,* and *ventilation.* I believe that *forgiveness* is the healthiest and the New Testament's answer to the problem of anger. I will discuss this last way of resolving anger in more detail in the next chapter, but the first three deserve some comment.

Repression of anger has always been known to be harmful. Repression is literally a putting down of the anger. It is holding back your anger and forcing it out of your awareness. You may even deny that it exists, causing even more problems. In repression you run the risk of developing such psychosomatic disorders as high blood pressure, tension headache, muscular fatigue, and gastric disturbances. It is psychologically and physically damaging because it disturbs your relationships with others and prevents you from getting at the real issues between yourself and other people. When you hold back your anger you do not eliminate it, but cause it to find other ways of expression. This can distort your perspective on important life issues and cause you to become cynical and miserable.

Of course, I am not advocating that one should give unrestrained expression to all one's anger. As you will see in due course, there is a big difference between expressing your anger in a destructive way and using it creatively and constructively.

Scapegoating refers to the tendency to take the anger that belongs in one place and dump it on another. The real source of the anger never receives the anger reaction. You find a much "safer" person or object to dump it on.

When you have been bawled out by your employer for some mistake and you cannot express your anger directly to him, you may go home and immediately find something to criticize in your wife or get angry at your kids. "Watch out, Mom, kids, cats and dogs! Here comes Dad and he is mad again!" This is how many families feel. I have heard this so often that I am convinced it is as American as apple pie!

Scapegoating is very common in relationships. So common, in fact, that we hardly ever recognize when it is taking place. I suppose it is only human to want to take out our anger on a "safer" person or object, but doing this day in and day out must eventually have a detrimental effect on our relatives and friends (not to mention our pets).

The origin of the term *scapegoating* is interesting and helps us clarify what we mean by this term. It comes from the Old Testament reference to the innocent goat which was brought to the altar by the High Priest (see Leviticus 16:20–22). Laying both hands on the goat's head, the High Priest confesses all the sins of the people. The goat is then taken out into the wilderness and allowed to go free, thus symbolically taking all the sins of all the people and carrying them into a land that is uninhabited. He is called the "scapegoat" which literally means the "escape" goat. It's not the goat that escapes, but the people!

Don't you feel like this goat at times? Innocent. You have done nothing wrong. Suddenly you become the recipient of a lot of undeserved anger. It is heaped on your head by your wife or husband, your adolescent child, a parent, or a friend. You know you didn't cause the hurt. Why do they then get angry with you? Why can't they direct their anger at the real source of the hurt? Worse still, they won't even acknowledge that they are really angry at someone else. You don't even have the relief of being able to run away to an uninhabited country where you start all over again!

This is the trap in which many find themselves. Much misery and many disturbed relationships are caused by inappropriate scapegoating of anger. If you do this, take heart; it's not that difficult to change. I know—because I've been able to! Part of the problem is solved just by admitting that this is what you do. The rest comes from paying careful attention to the ideas I will present in the next chapter.

Ventilation is the term used by many psychologists to describe what they consider to be the best method for resolving anger. Those who advocate this method take the view that it is desirable (and even a dire necessity) that we let all our angry feelings and hostility "out," whenever we can. They insist that it is bad to bottle up anger and that good only comes from "attacking" the source of your anger with words, foam-rubber bats, and tennis rackets—whatever is at hand.

Some parents who have accepted this idea allow their children to cut up and destroy their toys, throw stones at others, and even encourage their children to go to their bedrooms and scream their heads off. They believe that the discharge of pent-up anger is beneficial and that the urge to destroy is normal and necessary, and it must even be encouraged.

My instinct and my understanding of the gospel's message tells me that there is something wrong with this approach. I began as a therapist using lots of ventilation—but people didn't get better, they got angrier. I have worked in therapy with enough angry people to know that while the expression of anger in open and aggressive ways seems to be emotionally satisfying, it neither removes the cause for the anger nor drains away the angry feelings. Above all, this approach does not help people to come to terms with their frustration proneness nor does it teach them how to heal their hurts.

There is ample experimental evidence to show that such "ventilation" techniques for dealing with anger (where one allows the anger to express itself in violent words and actions) only serves to reduce controls against anger and encourages more frequent use of aggressive behavior in venting anger feelings.

Also, there is much secondary benefit to be derived from expressing anger. Adrenalin flows strong and one feels good—at the time! But this does not cure the anger problem.

One study showed that children who were originally low in aggressive behavior and who were given free-play experiences with aggressive toys became significantly more aggressive in their behavior *after* playing with these toys. Presumably this was because the aggressive make-believe activity lowered their normal restraints against aggression. Playing with aggressive toys does not drain away anger. Rather, it opens up new ways for expressing anger and for translating anger into hostility. Aggressive behavior is, in many respects, self-rewarding and inherently satisfying, so that it can easily become entrenched as a behavior style without serving any anger-release advantages whatsoever.

Ventilation techniques for resolving anger appear to be effective because of one simple effect: when you translate anger (as a feeling) into aggression and hostility (behavior), it seems to relieve the anger. I think it is very important to make a distinction between *anger* (the *feeling* component) and *aggression and hostility* (the *behavior* which expresses the anger). By transforming anger (the feeling) into hostility (the behavior arising from the feeling), we provide a way for resolving the anger. But anger (as feeling) can be dealt with *before* it becomes aggression.

It has been shown experimentally that when anger is provoked, blood pressure is elevated. If the object causing the anger is attacked, blood pressure rapidly decreases. If no attack is allowed and the person is left alone, it takes much longer for the pressure to return to normal. The translation of the angry feeling into an action of attack provides relief from the feeling as well as from the consequent physiological reaction. It is this mechanism which is utilized when one encourages someone to "ventilate" anger and express it in action.

But is this the only way to resolve angry feelings? Does this not ignore the long-term effects of these expressive actions? Would this behavior not create further conflict in the environment of those around, such that further anger is generated by their counter-reactions?

I once had a woman come to me after a lecture I had given on "The Christian and Anger" and tell me about her best friend's eighteen-year-old daughter who had been in therapy for two years. The teenager was somewhat withdrawn and passive in her personality when she first started psychotherapy, but shortly after she commenced, she became a very hostile and angry person. At the insistence of her therapist she began lashing out angrily at everyone around her. She found this behavior so rewarding that after two years it had become an established personality style with her. Unfortunately, neither her mother, her mother's friend who related the story to me, nor anyone else in the girl's life found this to be pleasant. She was soon ostracized by all her friends.

The question that this woman posed to me was: "Is she better off after such therapy than she would have been if left as she was?" I could not say with any certainty whether she would have been better without the therapy, but I do know that there is a better way to deal with anger than to translate it into hostility and aggression.

This is not to say that there are no therapeutic benefits to be derived from the use of ventilation techniques. These techniques, used carefully and under the supervision of an experienced therapist, can speed up therapy and bring much needed relief to those who cannot cope with their anger. However, they should only be used by trained professionals, as there is a high probability that the person so helped will act aggressively outside the therapy setting as well. What is, therefore, a very effective therapeutic technique should be contained within the therapy situation and should not be allowed to become a normal style for everyday living. A legitimate and effective therapeutic technique is not necessarily a legitimate lifestyle.

Anger and the Gospel

The need to differentiate between *anger* (the feeling) and *hostility/aggression* (the behavior arising out of the feeling) is even more important when we turn to understanding the New Testament's approach to the problem of anger. The apostle Paul presents us with what at first seems to be an impossible paradox: "Be ye angry, and sin not: let not the sun go down upon your wrath" (Ephesians 4:26 KJV).

How can one be angry and not sin? The New English Bible translation makes a little clearer what the apostle Paul was saying and provides us with a very up-to-date understanding, not only of the nature of anger, but also of its solution: "If you are angry, do not let anger lead you into sin; do not let the sunset find you still nursing it. . . ."

My understanding of what Paul is saying here is that it is not the anger itself (as feeling) that is wrong, but that since angry feelings have the potential for becoming angry behavior, it can lead you into sin. It is the *translation* or conversion of anger feelings, aggressive and hostile acts, that leads to sin. To *feel* anger, to tell someone that you feel angry, and to talk about your feeling of anger is healthy and necessary. This is because the *feeling* of anger is a signal—a warning sign if you prefer—that a violation has taken place. As long as you recognize the anger as your own and avoid hurting the object of your anger, you are keeping it as a feeling—and *all* feelings are legitimate! What you *do* with your feeling may not be, and this is where you can fall into sin!

The context of Paul's injunction makes his intention very clear. Both here in Ephesians 4, as well as in Romans 12 (where he deals with the revengeful aspects of anger), the need for the control of anger (as behavior) is placed in the context of the need for unity in "the body of Christ." In the immediately preceding verse, he tells us, "Then throw off falsehood; speak the truth to each other, for all of us are the parts of one body" (Ephesians 4:25 NEB). The need for harmony within the body dictates that anger must somehow be controlled or channeled into nondestructive outlets. Whether the "body" is the church, as Paul intends here, or the home, or the office, harmonious relationships are only possible where there is a healthy anger recognition (as feeling), freedom to talk about this feeling, but constraint over how it is exposed in hurtful and aggressive acts. Nothing is more destructive to relationships than anger that has been uncontrollably transformed into hostile and aggressive actions.

The reasons why anger has so much potential for "leading us into sin" are not difficult to identify:

1. *Our lower nature wants revenge.* I will deal with this more fully in the next chapter, but let me point out here that anger which is the result of hurt is often, if not always, accompanied by a strong desire to take revenge and obtain satisfaction from the one who has hurt us. This "response tendency" is built into us. That is why Paul has to admonish us: "Never pay back evil for evil . . . . If possible, so far as it lies with you, live at peace with all men. My dear friends, *do not seek revenge. . .* (Romans 12:17–19 NEB; italics added).

While we have difficulty admitting we love revenge, our attitude toward those who hurt us betrays us every time.

2. *The emotion of anger is a very powerful controller of our behavior.* Anger has potential for sin because when we are angry we lose control of ourselves. We can then no longer be responsible for what we do. Anger takes over like a hurricane and determines the direction we go. Our tiny self-control rudder has little effect when the raging force of anger controls us. Men have been known to commit murder under such conditions, and we are very naive if we do not recognize the power of anger to take control of what we do and say.

3. *Anger blocks our ability to love.* Above all else, we are commanded to love one another. We cannot do this when we are given to angry behavior. Anger will motivate us to hate, wound, damage, despise, curse, scold and humiliate. We cannot love under these conditions, and everything we stand for is in danger of being destroyed when we allow anger to be transformed into hostile words and actions.

An emotion with the potential for so much sin needs to be avoided as much as possible. Anger (as feeling) may be inevitable in our lives, and we certainly must be aware of it and accept it as a normal response whenever it occurs. To reduce its potential for sin, however, we must learn new ways of coping with this feeling. Especially, we must learn how not to trigger angry behavior and how to resolve it quickly. Paul sets a limit on the time available to do this: ". . . before sunset." How to resolve your anger feelings effectively and in a healthy way is the topic of the next chapter.

Summary

Even among psychologists, there is much confusion about the nature of anger and how best to deal with it. There is a constructive way to deal with angry feelings without causing discomfort to others and—for the Christian—without compromising one's faith.

Greater understanding of the mechanisms of anger can be attained through examining the origins of anger (biological and learned); its causes (frustration, hurt, conditioned response, instinctive protection); passive and direct methods of expression; and its resolution. The latter is represented most commonly by *repression, scapegoating,* and *ventilation.*

Although each of these mechanisms may provide some relief from the pressures of angry feelings, there are guidelines that can lead to more effective and healthy ways of handling this powerful emotion.

Additional Reading

1. *Making Anger Your Ally,* Neil Warren (New York: Doubleday).
2. *How to Get Angry Without Feeling Guilty,* Adelaide Bry (New York: New American Library).
3. *Anger,* Leo Madow (New York: Scribner's).
4. Ephesians 4.

5

Freedom from Anger

In the preceding chapter I stated that while there are many ways we can deal with our anger, *forgiveness* holds the most promise for aiding us to effectively resolve our feelings of anger. This concept is so important that I want to devote a chapter to showing how effective and central it is to a Christian understanding of how to deal with anger.

Forgiveness is at the heart of the Christian gospel. It is the "genius" and exclusive domain of Christianity, and not without reason. God knows who and what we are and He has given and demonstrated forgiveness in a remarkable way. He knows that we need to both give and receive forgiveness. As a psychologist I am convinced that to know both how to receive and give forgiveness is crucial to the problem of anger. No person is emotionally or spiritually mature who has not mastered the art of forgiving.

The Frustration of Unresolved Anger

There are many situations in which we will not be able to deal with our anger in any active way. Even if we could discuss our feelings with those who are causing hurt and anger, we cannot always have the satisfaction of an apology or a clearing up of some misunderstanding. Our feelings will frequently be left "in the air" with no hope of working them through with those concerned. Often the person causing the anger is inaccessible to us. It may be an employer, or the person may have died. How do we get satisfaction and resolve our anger in such cases? As I have already pointed out, transforming one's anger into hostility or aggression may help if it is done under controlled therapeutic conditions, but only a few have this opportunity available to them.

I will try to show that when we are trapped by such an impasse there is only one course of action open to us. This course has been clearly charted for us in the New Testament writings and can be summed up in the concept of "forgiveness." I urge you to come to terms with it. Find out for yourself how freeing it can be for you to experience it, and learn how to be an effective forgiver.

Don't think for one moment that it is easy. You need to understand forgiveness in the context of a number of other important concepts and needs, and these must all be woven into the total fabric if you are going to resolve your anger quickly.

Cut Off Your Anger at the Earliest Possible Moment

Before we look at the steps involved in resolving anger, let me stress how important it is to try and cut off your anger at the earliest possible moment, preferably at the trigger point. Again and again I find that clients don't realize what tremendous ability they have to *avoid* getting angry in the first place. Quite recently a client told me that for many years her husband was able to make her extremely angry, always over the same incident. It would be breaking a confidence to reveal the specific details, but again and again the same incident caused her to become angry. Since it occurred with such regularity (and there was nothing she could do to change her husband's behavior), I asked my client why she continued to give this incident the power to make her angry. I reminded her that she was responsible for her reactions and that she could stop becoming angry if she wanted to, merely by changing her attitude. It was her husband's problem, I insisted, and she did not have to make it hers. She was able to make some changes in her attitude, and the frequency of her anger reactions dropped dramatically. This paved the way for improved communication with her husband, and the marital relationship also showed a dramatic turn for the better.

This story is by no means unusual or rare. We get angry without thinking about whether or not we could have avoided it. *All* anger has a point at which it begins (the trigger point), and there are many ways we can deal with our thoughts and attitudes either to avoid the trigger or to cut off the anger at the earliest possible moment. Let us explore some of these before we go much further.

You can deal with your anger at four different points:

1. When you are calm and not bothered by the anger.
2. Just before you respond in anger to some event.
3. Just after you have become angry, but before you have transformed the anger into hostility.
4. When your anger has turned to overt hostility.

1. Dealing with Anger in Your Sane Moments

When you are calm and peaceful is the best possible time to prepare yourself to deal with anger. Examine your recent *anger episodes* and honestly face up to whether you could have avoided them. Do you make unrealistic demands of others? Are you impatient and do you always want your own way? Do you set up unrealistic expectations or expect people to guess what you are thinking or wanting—and then get angry when they make a mistake?

If you have a low tolerance for frustration, you could work at raising this tolerance. You can remind yourself that you cannot always get your way. Others have rights also. People are only human. Motor mechanics *do* make mistakes and foul up repairs. Children *are* inconsiderate and inconsistent and don't necessarily change as they get older. Husbands *do* forget birthdays and anniversaries, and friends are *not always* considerate of your feelings. So why not build into your belief system and expectations some allowance for these common human inadequacies? Learn to be more tolerant of these imperfections. This will stop you from getting angry in the first place.

If you do this often, you will find that much of your anger is unnecessary and can be completely avoided with a little bit of forethought and a change in attitude.

Use your prayer time, meditation, or devotions to *upgrade* your tolerance for frustration and the imperfections of others. Chart your anger responses carefully and see whether you are getting angry over the same thing over and over again. If so, what is the reason? Ask: What can I change to stop this? Talk to the person who constantly thwarts you or puts you down. Explain to him or her how you react to their behavior and explore ways for preventing it from happening again. In sum, try to *remove the causes of your anger* while you are calm and objective and have all your resources at your disposal.

2. Cutting Off Anger Just Before It Happens

Even though you may have done your homework well during your sane moments, there will be times when anger will break through. (I can guarantee this!) Since life is full of frustrations and hurts, occasions for anger inevitably arise. Careful preparation of your attitudes, as I have outlined in the previous section, can help you here also.

Frequently you can see an anger episode coming. The signs are not difficult to miss. "There he goes again with his criticism." "She's going to nag me when I get home." "I wonder why he said that to me!" These are typical self-conversations just before we get angry. With a little thought you can prepare a list of these self-talk statements so that you can recognize them when they start. You can prepare yourself by asking: "Do I need to get angry? Will it help me to handle this issue better?" At this early stage you *do* have a choice. You can proceed to develop the anger through your self-talk or you can decide to deal with the problem some other way. By believing that you *have a choice* you can give yourself freedom not to get angry.

3. When You Are Angry

Assuming that you cannot avoid the trigger, what do you do with a fully developed anger feeling? First, *recognize and admit your anger*. It sounds so simple, doesn't it? Do you know how hard it is to acknowledge your anger *when* you are angry? The anger tends to block out any awareness of itself, almost as if it were "afraid" that, once recognized, it would have to go away. Most of us, I suspect, have a marked tendency to want to deny the presence of our anger. We see it as a sign of weakness or of being out of control.

If you don't know you are angry, it stands to reason that you cannot proceed to resolve it. If you resist acknowledging it, you will only aggravate the problem. To be angry and yet not own up to it makes you a very difficult person to be around. Is it any wonder then that others find it difficult to love you?

How can you improve your anger recognition? Pray for sensitivity and self-honesty. Contract with a friend, your spouse, or even a parent to tell you when they perceive you to be angry. Do not be concerned about whether the perception is right or wrong; just accept their input and examine your feeling. Your defense system may not allow you to admit to the anger, so you may need to find a way around it. Ignore your own denial and take at face value what the other is saying. You will soon discover if you are angry or not. Begin to open yourself to greater self-honesty.

This honesty only comes when you stop being defensive. You can only teach yourself to be less defensive when you accept as valid the perception that others have of you. If you are truly not angry when they say you are, you are none the worse, since even if you take the next steps, no harm can come of it. You will find it to be a good exercise for your soul. You are better off assuming that you are angry when others tell you that you are than continuing to stand your ground, denying and increasing your defensiveness.

Second, *release your vindictiveness.* Once you have admitted and owned up to your anger, the next step is to deal with your strong, almost inbuilt desire, to *hurt back* and obtain satisfaction from the offending party. Gone are the days when you can slap a gauntlet across your enemy's face and challenge him to a duel!

I must stress that this need to hurt back is present *every time* you are angered by hurt. It can take a subtle form so that you may not be able to recognize it. Your need to deny may be stronger than your need to get revenge. But it *is* there and must be dealt with before you can lay aside your anger.

It is a law of our lower nature that we want to hurt back when we are hurt. It probably serves some protective function, and in more primitive settings it makes survival possible. It becomes a much more subtle exercise in our modern society and doesn't always involve physical retaliation. Invariably we use psychological strategies for taking revenge.

We can see this law at work in the development of our children. When they are very young they fight back every time they are hurt. It is as if their survival depends on it. At first it is merely a physical defense, but later it becomes a desire to hurt back in order to "even the score." Much later in life, of course, we learn how to psychologize the hurting back and substitute words for actions, and psychological pain for physical pain.

The portion of the Sermon on the Mount found in Matthew 5:38–48 is most illuminating on this point and provides us with some important insight for dealing with anger. Read this portion of Scripture again in your favorite translation.

Jesus is discussing our relationship to our enemies. Who are our enemies? Anyone who has the potential to hurt us! It can be a husband, a parent, or a friend, just as easily as the person at work who dislikes you. Don't think of your enemy as only someone who is at war with you. Rather, it can be someone very close to you.

How should you deal with your enemy—that person who has the potential to hurt you? You can easily misunderstand the point of what Jesus is saying if you focus too much on your enemy "getting away with it." We are so afraid that someone who hurts us will not get punished. "If I let him get away with that, he won't respect me and will do it to me over and over again!" This reaction highlights the fact that we are often too preoccupied with "balancing the score" whenever we are hurt. From time to time I have received a citation for speeding. I don't intend to speed, but you know how it is—you don't always keep an eye on the speedometer! When I get a speeding ticket, I become angry, even though I know I am guilty. I direct my anger at the officer and my self-talk goes something like this: "Why does he waste his time speed-trapping? Aren't there real criminals out there? How can I get back at him?" Ridiculous, of course, but this is how I react when I'm angry. I suspect you do too.

Now what Jesus is saying to us in the Sermon on the Mount is simply that this is what we are like. The old law says we can take "an eye for an eye and a tooth for a tooth." This law follows our basic instincts and lets us do what we deep down want to do—take revenge. But God knows that this natural tendency to want revenge is so strong and overpowering that we will not know when to stop. Can we be content taking just one eye? I doubt it. God knows it. When we punish, we always go too far to even the score.

History has taught us this lesson. Vigilante groups, feuds, and lynching mobs all bear testimony to the fact that the old law failed because no one who is hurt can restrain himself and limit the revenge to an exact "eye for eye." So Jesus has to tell us to "turn the other cheek" and "go the extra mile." In so doing He is *not* telling us to give our enemy some advantage over us. He is doing this for our protection.

In effect He is saying, "Because you do not know what real justice is, I cannot trust you with punishment. When someone hurts you, you are better off letting him hurt you again than trying to hurt him back. You don't know when to stop."

"Cheek turning," therefore, is not for our enemy's advantage, but for our own protection. If we do not follow this principle, when we have finished punishing our enemy he will only be ready to take his turn at punishing us back—and the cycle repeats itself over and over again. When such a cycle gets out of hand we call it "war."

The principle of "cheek turning" is so important that we need to apply it even to when we discipline our children. *Every* act of discipline can be seen as compromising one part of us that wants revenge with a need to correct the faulty behavior. Our need to punish is often jumbled up with the need to correct behavior. There is a very important difference then between "punishment" and "discipline." Punishment is heavy on revenge. Discipline should be free of revenge.

When the need to punish is greater than the need to discipline, we have the situation depicted in Figure 2 (see p. 64). The need to "hurt back" is greater than the need to correct the behavior.

If we are overly angry when we try to discipline, we may not be correcting the faulty behavior at all. We may only be creating resentment and setting up so much anger and hostility as a reaction in the child, that his need to hurt back prevents him from experiencing any effective learning. This is a major cause of teenage rebellion. By careful design of our discipline procedures we should be able to reduce the contribution of the need to punish or hurt back and

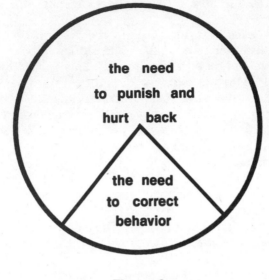

Figure 2

Discipline with Too Much Punishment

maximize the need for correction. Correct discipline would look like Figure 3.

How do we achieve this? By doing exactly what we would do to *anyone* hurting us. We must first free ourselves of any vindictiveness and desire to hurt back. This is the essence of what Jesus is saying in Matthew 5.

"Cheek turning" does not mean that we become doormats and let everyone trample over us. "Cheek turning" is not intended to be an act of surrender or capitulation, nor is it meant to perpetuate domination by one person over another. Neither is it intended to be the "behavior of confusion," in which one does not have the ability to stand up for oneself. It is simply a recognition of who we are and what we are capable of when taking revenge. When we are hurt we have a very strong urge to hurt back. God asks us to set this urge aside and leave all punishment to Him.

There is ample evidence in the history of humankind (as well as in our own personal history, I am sure) that when we hurt back we do not know when to stop. The Old Testament's principle of "an eye for an eye and a tooth for a tooth" is difficult to put into practice when *you* are the one who is hurting. We cannot tell when the scales are balanced and when to stop. God has therefore set down

Figure 3

The Correct Way to Discipline

this principle which Paul also emphasizes in Romans: "Never pay back evil for evil. Let your aims be such as all men count honorable. If possible, so far as it lies with you, live at peace with all men. My dear friends, do not seek revenge, but leave a place for divine retribution. . . " (Romans 12:17–19 NEB).

But how do we give up this need to hurt back? Paul is very clear in Ephesians 4 on how to do this. After reminding us in verse 26 about anger's potential for sin, he proceeds to say: "Have done with spite and passion, all angry shouting and cursing, and bad feeling of every kind. Be generous to one another, tender-hearted, *forgiving* one another as God in Christ forgave you" (vv. 31, 32 NEB italics added).

Forgiveness is the key to giving up your need to hurt back. *Forgiveness* is the antidote for hurt anger. There is no other satisfactory solution to our urge to take revenge.

What is forgiveness? I am often asked this. In the context of the Scripture portions I have already cited, I would define *forgiveness* as follows: forgiveness is surrendering my right to hurt you back if you hurt me.

Print this in large letters and stick it on your bedroom mirror to remind you of it each day. I can confidently say that you will not be free of anger until you have learned how to put this into practice. I would even go further and say that under no circumstances should you confront someone else about your anger until you have *first* taken the step of forgiving and surrendering your right to hurt back. Your need for revenge will be too strong and will disrupt your attempt to get resolution.

Revenge also takes many subtle forms. You will only humiliate and embarrass the one who has hurt you if you don't first forgive. Just asking someone to admit that they have hurt you and to apologize can be seen as a "hurting back" maneuver. By insisting that the other person apologize, you cause them the pain of humiliation.

This is how "hurting back" works to resolve your anger. You have to hurt the other person a little more than you've been hurt so that you begin to feel guilty. The guilt replaces the anger—and balance is restored. Unfortunately, the other person now feels violated and has a need to hurt you again. So the cycle goes on repeating itself. Forgiveness interrupts this cycle.

Some may be thinking right now: *Yes, this all sounds so easy. But putting it into practice is another matter.* I agree, it *is* difficult to be forgiving, but this doesn't mean it isn't the right way. I know of no more effective motivation for forgiving than the remembrance of God's forgiveness toward us through Christ. Remind yourself that forgiving others is not just optional but mandatory. Jesus taught us to pray "And forgive us our debts, as we forgive our debtors" (Matthew 6:12 NEB). These "debts" are debts of hurt. Your forgiveness from God is contingent upon your willingness to forgive others. Furthermore, to forgive another is for *your* benefit, not for the one who is being forgiven. Don't get hung up on your enemy getting away with some advantage over you. Forgiving is for your benefit, not your enemy's! You are the one who is set free—set free from revenge and hatred.

It has been my sad experience to observe that many Christians who claim to have received God's forgiveness know little of how to forgive others. By some strange logic they exclude anyone who has hurt them from the list of those to whom they should now have a forgiving attitude. I know wives who cannot forgive husbands, children their parents, and workers their bosses. I know pastors who bear deep resentment toward their churches. We need, it seems, to be trained in the "art of forgiveness." I have often considered setting up therapy groups specifically designed to deal with issues of forgiving, and I have heard of many such groups all around the country. We need to be taught how to forgive, and I think that such training could revolutionize relationships. Our homes, churches, and work situations can be transformed by a little touch of forgiving.

The *third* step in handling angry feelings is to *express the anger.* This step can only be taken after the first two, especially after you have surrendered your vindictiveness. If someone has angered or continues to anger you, it may be necessary for you to reflect this anger directly to the person concerned and *talk* about it. It is far better to do this than to continue harboring the unexpressed anger feeling and allow it to influence your relationship in negative ways.

However, in expressing your anger there are a number of rules you should follow:

• *Try to deal with your hurts and anger as they arise, one at a time.* In other words, keep short accounts. This may mean you must be more assertive and develop the courage to face those who hurt you. If you are not strong and honestly assertive, you accumulate hurts. Often the only time we are assertive is when we are angry. This is *not* the way to be assertive. A Christian assertiveness is, above all, honest and loving. So try to assert yourself *before* you get angry. Once your anger has been transformed into hostility and aggression you are hardly in a good position to talk about it objectively.

• *Accept responsibility for your anger.* It is *your* feeling, and there is no point in trying to force the other person into accepting blame for it. Your anger may not even be justified and could be due to some misunderstanding. Do not blame others for how you feel. Accept responsibility for it and then you are ready to deal with it constructively.

• *Acknowledge the right of the other person to have feelings also.* Anger is seldom a one-way street. If someone hurts you it is because he or she is angry also. As you approach this person about your anger, you could easily cause an anger reaction in him or her. Be prepared for it—and give the other person the right also to feel hurt.

• *Listen, receive, and accept any explanation of apology that may be offered.* Accept it gracefully and thankfully if it is offered. Do not try to force an apology out of the other person if it is not. Your goal should be to facilitate clear communication about the nature of your anger and what is causing it, not to humiliate the other person.

• *Make a goal of trying to get understanding between the two of you, not necessarily agreement.* This is probably the most difficult step. You may need to keep going back to the place of forgiveness again and again. You may never get the other person to agree with the reason for your anger, but if you can achieve some mutual *understanding,* you will have accomplished your goal. Your desire should be to help clear up the effect his or her action is having on you and how this causes you to feel hurt. If you have successfully moved yourself to an attitude and willingness to forgive, understanding should come easily. Not only will you resolve your anger but you will also deepen the intimacy of your relationship with the offending person.

"Expressing" your anger is an important step if you are generally not an assertive person. If you cannot easily call a halt when you are being hurt or if you allow people to run all over you, you may need to improve your assertiveness skills and learn how to express your hurt feelings more directly. As I have tried to show, "turning the other cheek" is an act of forgiveness. It does not preclude you from talking to the offending person about your feelings. Don't use "cheek turning" as an excuse to hide your lack of assertiveness.

4. When Anger Has Become Hostility

This is the last opportunity to cut off your anger, when your anger has found expression in some hostile act or behavior. To begin with, you must be honest enough to admit that you have crossed the line from feeling (which is legitimate) to behavior (which has potential for sin). Your goal at this point must be to retreat, as rapidly as you can, to the *feeling* state and deal with it in terms of forgiveness. In other words, pull back from your actions. Now is the time to count to one hundred and leave the scene of your anger. Retreat to a safer place! If you have already retaliated and created hurt in the other person, you should take steps to remedy this. It takes an honest and mature person to admit blame. Forget about your hurt and apologize for the hurt you are now causing.

At this point the problem is now yours—no matter how legitimate you may feel your anger was originally and how wrong the other person was. It is no longer the other's reaction that is at fault, but yours. The sooner you can remedy the situation by apologizing and withdrawing your punishment or whatever else you may be doing, the better. You can then retreat to the step of forgiving, and until you have conquered your need for revenge, don't proceed.

Developing a Perspective on Your Hurts

Life is full of potential for hurt and thus can create anger at every turn. It is inevitable that we will be hurt by *people* and by *circumstances*. People hurt us *because* they are human. They make mistakes; they are selfish and self-centered; they demand perfection and are intolerant of our mistakes. In fact, they are just as human as we are!

We can be hurt by circumstances over which we have no control. We can become ill with cancer or paralyzed in an accident. Some circumstances can be avoided, but we are often caught unawares and suffer the consequences of unjust acts by others.

The potential for being hurt is there all the time. If we allow all these hurts to create anger in us every time they occur, we will never be free and happy.

When anger remains unresolved over a long period of time, it creates a feeling of displeasure and indignation which is called "resentment," and this resentment is a powerful controller of other emotions and behaviors. Resentment can create and maintain a strong need for revenge that can become a grudge we carry for a long period of time. Some people carry grudges all their lives, postponing revenge almost indefinitely. These scars of resentment can often only be unearthed in therapy, and I have encountered very elderly people who have carried resentments about their hurts all their lives and have been unable to get rid of them. This has robbed them of happiness and caused them to become bitter and full of misery.

Carrying resentment for such a long time can easily take its toll on physical and mental life. It causes ulcers, high blood pressure, and a host of other minor and major ailments. Psychologically, these people become unattractive and difficult to relate to; they develop an angry personality, spend their life and collect "hurt stamps," and create chips on their shoulders. They live for the day when they will be able to cash in their books and satisfy their need for revenge.

Resentment is hard to recognize, isn't it? It eludes awareness and somehow remains camouflaged. Whenever someone else notices it, you jump to its defense by saying, "But I have suffered. I have a right to feel resentful." You become sensitive and touchy. You are suspicious of what others think and say. You are very selective in what you hear and distort what you see so as to feed your hurts and maintain your resentment. Is this how God intended us to live? I hope not! I doubt whether anyone can be happy who is full of resentment.

To help you put resentments in proper perspective, Jesus told an important parable in Matthew 18:21–35. It was after the Transfiguration and He was about to leave Galilee and move on to Capernaum and Jerusalem where He knew He would have to face the prospect of the Cross. Peter asked Jesus, "Lord, how often am I to forgive my brother if he wrongs me?" Jesus then told the parable of the king who decided to settle all his accounts. One servant had a debt of a million dollars, so to speak. This servant, pleading for mercy, promises to pay it all as soon as possible. The king is moved to mercy and forgives the servant's debt, every cent of it, despite the servant's offer to pay it back sooner or later. This same servant, shortly after, encounters another servant who owes him the equivalent of ten dollars. He demands that the debt be paid. The second servant makes the same offer to repay as the first had made to the king, but it is refused and the first servant has him jailed until the debt is paid. This distresses all the other servants and so they tell the king. He becomes furious! Calling the first servant back he says: "I forgave you all your debt. Should you not have had the same compassion on your fellow servant?"

Jesus ends the parable with these words: "And so angry was the master that he condemned the man to torture until he should pay the debt in full. And this is how my heavenly Father will deal with you, unless you each forgive your brother from your hearts" (Matthew 18:34, 35 NEB).

This is an alarming parable when you reflect on it. Its message is very clear. You cannot miss the essential truth of what Jesus is saying. It is not a parable about money, but about resentment—about the sins committed against you (see verse 21). In essence He is reminding us that we owe God more than we owe anyone else because we have sinned against God *more* than others have sinned against us. We have caused God more hurt than any other person has ever caused us (the ratio is about 200,000 to 1, if I am to take the parable literally). If God therefore forgives us, what right have we not to forgive those who hurt us?

We so easily suffer from "hurt myopia," a disorder in which we always see the hurts we cause others as being smaller than the hurts they cause us. Have you thought about the hurts you cause God by your waywardness and disobedience? This reflection, if you allow it to filter down to the depths of your being, can liberate you from the prison of resentment and allow you to experience and live in the freedom of forgiveness, both from God and toward others. All this is possible because He *first* forgave you.

Can Anger Accumulate?

In drawing my discussion of anger to a close I need to comment on another aspect of anger, as it relates to forgiveness. You often hear psychologists talk about how anger "builds up" or "accumulates." Implied in this idea is the belief that, anger is somehow stored somewhere, and must therefore be "drained away." While these terms may well describe how it feels to an angry person when anger is experienced over a period of time, they are quite erroneous and misleading, and can even be damaging.

The basic fact is that anger does *not* accumulate, as I have said before. Nowhere in the body can it be stored up.

One of my clients literally believed that all his anger went into a large reservoir and was kept there until such time as it could be drained. This mental image haunted him. He began to fear what would happen when his "reservoir of anger" became so full that it would burst. What was even more damaging was his belief that he had to drain his anger by becoming violent, screaming, and breaking things. His belief allowed him no other way to get rid of his anger. He patiently waited for a time and opportunity when he could "pull the plug" and let it all go. Needless to say, this belief about the nature of his anger was more damaging to him than the anger itself.

The idea that anger can accumulate is quite common. It originates in the "energy" theory of anger. This theory supposes that every time we get angry we build up a state of tension within ourselves. The energy of this tension is then stored and must be "discharged" before the anger will subside. As proof that this is what happens, these theorists point to the fact that we experience relief from anger whenever we lash out at its source.

As I have tried to show, lashing out is merely a way of transforming anger into hostility. This satisfies our need to hurt back and restores our anger reaction to normal. But the notion of "stored" anger is misleading. While it may appear that you are draining some of your dammed-up anger when you become hostile and aggressive, this apparent relief does not prove that anything is actually stored. All you are doing is resetting your body to a nonaggressive state of arousal.

I prefer to describe anger as an emotion that is always in the "here and now." This is true of all emotions. They can only exist in the present. I cannot experience yesterday's anger today anymore than I experience yesterday's happiness today. To be correct, what we do "store" are the memories of hurts, the resentments, that have the ability to *recreate* anger in us in the present.

If a friend said something to me last week that was hurtful and made me extremely angry, it is not last week's anger that I am experiencing today as I reflect upon the hurt. It is the *memory* of the hurtful comment that continues to recreate that anger in me in the present. Only memories are stored, not emotions.

This idea has important implications for how we should deal with anger. If memories are the problem, then it means that we only have to deal with these memories to dispose of our resentments. If we can take the sting out of them, we will remove their power to retrigger our anger in the present. How can we do this? Obviously we cannot forget everything hurtful that has ever happened to us. "Forgive and forget" is trite and simplistic. I cannot, nor do I need to, forget. All I have to do is forgive. If I have forgotten the hurt, I don't need to forgive.

The solution lies in breaking the *power* of memories to recreate hurts at some later date. To do this you will have to "challenge" your memories. It may mean that you will have to recall certain hurtful episodes in your life. Did someone actually say what you think he said, or did you imagine it? Did this person intend to hurt you? Could you have some other reason for feeling hurt? By carefully exploring your hurt memories in this way, you can begin their healing and reduce their ability to bother you.

Even after you have done all of this, there will be some memories you can do nothing about; you will have to move yourself to the place of forgiveness. If someone has deliberately and maliciously hurt you, what else can you do but forgive? This is where you will need God's power. There are some things we cannot do by ourselves. God helps us do them. Forgiving is definitely one of those things.

Jesus and Anger

I cannot close this chapter without commenting on what I believe to be the most erroneous idea of all about anger—the use of Jesus' anger to justify feelings of anger. You must often hear the comment, as I do, that since Jesus got angry I have a right to get angry also. I can't believe how often well-meaning Christians say this to me.

When we make such a comment we forget to make an important distinction between anger as *feeling* and anger as *hostility and aggression*. Portions of Scripture (John 2:13–17; Matthew 23:13–39) which describe Jesus as getting angry are often used, in my opinion, merely to justify the perpetuation of a need to hurt someone back. In fact, nowhere does it say here that Jesus was angry. We infer this from His behavior. It is a "cover" for our own hostility. Some would even go so far as to use it to justify their many angry outbursts. One pastor I know, who became angry almost every day of his life, would often say: "I'm only doing what Jesus would have done in my position." I think he's wrong. Angry behavior is seldom necessary and almost always destructive.

While I accept that "true" anger, and by this I mean *just* the feeling of anger, is legitimate and quite normal, I am strongly of the opinion that it is better if you never get angry. Angry feelings are important signals of a violation, but these feelings should be heeded and disposed of quickly. I don't mean to imply that we should deny or suppress our anger. If we can cut off anger at the earliest possible moment, we will be much happier and healthier.

Those who hide behind Jesus' anger as a justification for their own, fail to realize that if Jesus ever became angry, He could do so without any need for revenge. His anger was directed at sin, not people. He always acted in the best interests of those He came to save and never had any desire to take revenge for personal hurt. His anger was *always* an expression of His love. If He became angry, He did so in response to the hurt which people were causing themselves, not Him. Mark 3:5 makes this point clearly: "And when he had looked round about with anger, being grieved for the hardness of their hearts. . ." (KJV). Jesus' anger is *not* the same as ours.

It is my opinion that we are seldom so totally free of selfish involvement and personal hurt that we can justify angry behavior. We do it—but we must recognize it as sin. We all have the potential for transforming angry feelings into hostility and aggression, and consequently we will always be potentially in need of forgiveness for this sin. This was *not* true of Jesus. Comparing His anger with ours only leads to erroneous and misleading conclusions.

Jesus demonstrated to us that anger can be dealt with constructively. If we could get angry only at what Jesus got angry at, we would make a wonderful world.

There are those who claim that their anger is "righteous indignation." In other words, to fight injustice in this world they believe they need to become angry over some issue and get others to be angry as well. Many good causes have had their beginning in someone getting angry and saying, "I'm going to do something about this injustice."

I applaud this. Often it does take the "signal" of anger to tell us that human and personal rights are being violated and that action is needed. However, we are talking here about anger as "feeling," and it always plays a necessary and normal role in mobilizing us to action.

What we must not do is build a system of altruism or justice on anger only. Once we know there is a violation of rights our actions need to be determined by rational and effective actions, not by wild and erratic anger outbursts. Anger's role is to warn us of wrongdoing and only in some instances to guide our counterattack. It is not to become a lifestyle—unless we seek our self-destruction.

Summary

If you can avoid getting angry, you are in a better position to cope with your world than if you allow yourself to become angry. The "feeling" of anger is not harmful, provided it is not turned into angry behavior, and it is resolved quickly. Undealt with, it has the potential for being transformed into hostility and hence becomes sin. Anger is an important signal, warning us of violation of our rights. Knowing how to forgive others by surrendering our right to hurt them back is the most effective way for resolving anger. God calls us to be for-givers, not attackers. Whenever possible, forgive first, then express and talk about your angry feelings to those who are causing them. Never try to justify anger. Try to be as free of it as you can.

Additional Reading

1. *The Freedom of Forgiveness,* David Augsburger (Chicago: Moody Press).
2. *Forgive and Forget,* Lewis Smedes (New York: Harper and Row).
3. *Freedom from Guilt,* Bruce Narramore and Bill Counts (Irvine, California: Harvest House).
4. Matthew 5:38–48; 18:21–35.

6

Freedom from Depression

Depression is one of the most complicated of all our emotions. It is complicated because it usually invokes other emotions as well, and because it can range in intensity from a mild feeling of the blues to one of the severest of all mental disorders requiring hospitalization. Since depression is a major cause of suicide, it cannot be ignored. It is also the most commonly experienced unpleasant emotion and inflicts itself upon all of us at some time or another in our lives, with a large percentage of the population experiencing some depression as a daily occurrence.

Interest in the problem of depression has risen sharply over the last few decades, especially since it appears that more people are suffering from depression now than ever before. This is, I believe, a reflection on the lifestyles we are developing in our western culture and the general loss of meaning and purpose in life that many are experiencing. The more affluent and secure we have become, the more boredom becomes a problem and the more prone we are to seek ways of escape through drugs and alcohol (which are the most common forms of self-treatment for depression).

Whatever our station in life and regardless of our age or sex, none of us can claim to be totally free of depression. Some, fortunately, do not experience it as often as others, and many who claim to be depression free are probably just not able to recognize its symptoms.

A Timeless, Universal Problem

It can be most comforting to realize that depression is as old as the human race. There is ample evidence that since the beginning of human history, humankind has experienced depression. It appears to be built into our bodies and, as we will see later, serves a very important protective function.

The first clear clinical description of depression comes to us from

75

Hippocrates in the fourth century B.C., and it sounds like an extract from a modern textbook on abnormal psychology. Hippocrates gives prominence to problems of love as a cause of depression, and both the Greeks and Romans held the view that all depression was caused by disappointments in love. Our teenage population might very well agree with this analysis!

The Bible also gives at least two clear descriptions of depression. In the story of King Ahab (1 Kings 21) when he could not have Naboth's vineyards, we are told that King Ahab ". . . turned away his face, and would eat no bread" (v. 4 KJV). This reaction is typical of depression, and this pattern has not changed at all these thousands of years. And then there was Elijah the Prophet who had had such a victory over the prophets of Baal on Mount Carmel (1 Kings 18). He prayed and fire came down and consumed his offering, an obvious sign that God was on his side. He prayed again, and it rained. When it was all over he ran for his life into the wilderness and was overcome by a deep depression. Sitting under a juniper tree he prayed that God would let him die (1 Kings 19:4).

Here we see a very common reaction which often follows a period of extreme elation or exhilaration. Our adrenalin goes from high to low, and depression sets in. The depressing effects of an anticlimax are well known to all of us. Merely accepting this as a normal physiological reaction to overactivity can free one to take full advantage of the depression and allow the body to heal itself.

Not only has depression always been with us, but it is also a universal phenomenon. Go to any part of the world and wherever you find people, no matter what their cultural history, you will find depression. It may take different forms, but you cannot mistake its universality.

I was born and raised in Africa as a European and was exposed to many primitive cultures when growing up. In more primitive groups the element of guilt is notably absent from depression. The tendency in these cultures is for blame to be externalized and placed on evil forces, ancestors, or one's enemies. People tend, therefore, not to blame themselves for their failures. Not surprisingly, this has important implications for their mental health. As one observes the transition to a western culture, blame gradually becomes more self-directed and a strong tendency toward guilt develops. Consequently, there is a much greater guilt component in the depressions of western culture. With or without the guilt component, depression is still universal, and the problem is not so much how to avoid it as what to do with it when it comes.

A Word of Caution

At the outset I need to stress that there are *many* forms of depression. Depression is a complex emotion. Some depressions are caused by physical factors (such as poor sleeping or eating habits and fatigue) while others are due to biochemical disturbances or genetic factors. My discussion will focus primarily on those depressions that are psychological in nature. If you (or someone you know) is experiencing a prolonged or severe depression with serious immobilization and extensive loss of perspective, I would recommend that you seek professional help. There is little I can offer as "self-help" for a serious depression. Some forms of depression need special treatment, including anti-depressant medication, and one should not delay obtaining treatment simply because one fears drug addiction or the like. Anti-depressants are *not* addicting and under proper care there is little risk of serious side effects. There is no point in living a miserable life when help can be obtained so easily.

Our antidrug feelings are legitimate but not applicable here. Many severely depressed people avoid appropriate help because they fear becoming hooked on medication. If you have weak eyes, you don't hesitate to wear corrective glasses. If you suffer from diabetes, you take insulin. If you have a biochemical or genetic predisposition toward depression, you should feel just as much freedom in taking the proper treatment. Remember, though, that anti-depressant medications do nothing for psychological depression.

What Do We Know about Depression?

We are beset by many theories about depression. They range from seeing all depression as purely psychological to those which see the problem as entirely physiological. Most likely the truth lies somewhere between these two extremes. Most depressions can be understood to be an interaction between psychological and physiological factors. Any theory that is going to be helpful will have to take into consideration this interactive process.

Sometimes psychological factors trigger depression, but since our minds and bodies operate in unison the depression recruits glands and hormones to be a part of the experience. The depressive ideas cause our bodies to respond in a depressed way, producing changes in our stomach, respiration, heartbeat, and so on. Together *with* the thoughts, they constitute the total depression package.

This is why depression does not go away the moment the cause for the depression is removed. Our needs disturb body chemistry, and it takes time for it to restore itself. I am stressing this here because so often we forget to make allowances for our biological involvement in depression. The speed with which your system returns to normal will depend on a number of factors, including the depth of your depression (the deeper the depression, the longer it will take for your system to recover); the nature of your physiology (some of us have systems that require a longer recovery time than others); whether there are distracting factors (if you are recovering from a depression and find yourself taken up with some other engaging activity, you are likely to recover more rapidly than if your activity is not distracting). These factors all determine how quickly you will return to normal.

The implication of this is that you must come to understand and accept your particular and unique style of being depressed and learn how to adjust and make allowances for it.

The Cyclic Nature of Our Emotions

Physiological research has repeatedly shown us that emotions have a tendency to be "cyclical" in nature. We each have our own characteristic "cycle of emotionality." Periods of good feelings (elation) are followed by periods of bad feelings (depression), and these can repeat themselves over and over again under the direction of hormonal and other influences. Some people do not experience much variability. They seem to be the same all the time. Others show much variability. Their lows may be severe enough to incapacitate them. These cycles are quite normal, and a period of low mood is not necessarily "depression." Clinically speaking, we only apply this label to low moods that are more severe and somewhat incapacitating or emotionally disruptive.

The cyclical nature of our emotions must be accepted as normal. There is little you can do to control these ups and downs, except ensure that you develop healthy life patterns. They are caused by involuntary physiological rhythms or by the body fighting disease and building anti-bodies.

The menstrual cycle is one type of biological rhythm which influences emotional life, and while I do not believe in the simplistic views of those who try to explain these cycles through "biorhythms," there is enough evidence to show that biological cycles are present to some degree in all of us and that they influence our emotions. They *cannot* be predicted as easily as the peddlers of biorhythm charts claim, nor can your astrological sign have *any* influence on your emotions. These claims are patently fraudulent! The cycles are *not* fixed and constant but may vary just as the menstrual cycle of women may vary.

Fatigue, illness, virus infections of the body, and many other natural factors will influence your emotional cycles. There is no way you can predict them with any accuracy. You should, however, come to know your own characteristic cycle and learn when to "mark time" or slow down and await the return of your normal feelings. When you are in a "high" stage and feel elated, savor it; use it to good advantage; and accomplish those difficult tasks that are waiting to be done. In your low times try to ignore your feeling. Do not allow yourself to feel miserable or morose. Find some distraction and ride out the storm until your cycle returns to normal. Many attempted suicides and life-changing decisions are made at these biological "low periods." They are very much regretted afterward.

Depression As a Symptom and a Reaction

As I have already pointed out there are *many* forms of depression. The form I have just described is more biological than psychological in origin. What we typically label "depression" is a more severe mood disturbance which is triggered or maintained by psychological factors and is accompanied by an extensive loss of perspective and distortion of reality. Typical symptoms of depression include loss of appetite, loss of interest in one's surroundings or activities, lethargy, self-criticism and self-condemnation, and an overwhelming feeling of unworthiness. Many also report a wish to die. "I pray that God will take me home while I am sleeping," one lady said to me recently. This pretty well captures the essence of depression.

But depression is *both* a symptom and a reaction. As a *symptom* it can be a warning signal that something needs attention. Its function here is one of preservation. It is attempting to slow you down and disengage you from your environment so that you can pay attention to something that needs repair. You lose interest in what you are doing, withdraw from social contacts, and you may even want to withdraw from life. This creates the conditions for healing. Without such depression we would self-destruct.

Depression can also be a symptom accompanying many infections. It often accompanies influenza, or it can be part of more serious disease. The greatest mistake one can make when experiencing this type of depression is to ignore it. It is your ally, disengaging you from normal activities so that healing can take place.

Your depression is a symptom of your physical disease, but it is also a part of the healing process.

Depression is not just a symptom; it is also a *reaction* to some of life's experiences, and these depressions are often called "reactive." They arise in reaction to the way you receive and handle life's losses.

At this point I should distinguish between *reactive* and *neurotic* depressions. While many professionals believe that *all* reactive depressions are neurotic, I prefer to make a distinction between the two. The label "neurotic depression" is reserved for a much more elusive lifestyle, where one takes on all of life with a depressed mood. It is more a way of dealing with deep-seated anxiety than depression itself. In neurotic depression you disengage from life, you may sleep excessively and hibernate, all because you refuse to engage life. If you are this way, I strongly recommend that you seek professional help.

The depressive reactions which I will discuss in this chapter are not continuous but tend to come in spurts. Usually there is a "trigger," often the perception of some loss. Sometimes these reactive depressions disappear spontaneously after the loss has been grieved, although they may have been the cause of considerable pain at the time.

Depression As a Response to Loss

The key to understanding nearly all of the reactive depressions is to see them as a *response to a sense of loss*. If you can come to understand how this sense of loss is triggered and develop ways for evaluating the loss and dealing with its reality, you can learn to overcome such depressions. I have found the technique I will describe extremely effective, and you should find it quite easy to apply to your own life.

There are *four* types of losses which can trigger reactive depression: real losses, abstract losses, imagined losses, and threatened losses. A clear understanding of the distinction between each of these types of losses will help in the early recognition of your particular loss.

1. *Real Losses.* These are the easiest to identify. They involve the loss of some tangible object, person, or privilege. Examples include the loss of a job, the misplacing of some prized object, or the loss of (or mere separation from) someone you love very much. The person or object lost is real. I have experienced depressions ranging in severity from a mild low to where I have been extremely miserable, as I am sure you have, in response to losses such as dropping and breaking my camera, receiving a speeding ticket (where the ticket represents loss of both money and self-esteem), and when I first had to start wearing reading glasses (which represented the realization

that my eyesight was being "lost" as I grew older). These are all *real losses* because they are tangible. They can be seen and handled.

The list of potential real losses is very long! Since we are tied to a material world, it is inevitable that we will experience many losses. The more we are tied to this world, the more we will experience real loss. The success with which we can deal with our depressions will depend to a great extent on our ability to develop a proper perspective on worldly possessions and objects. I will discuss this further when we look at the Christian's resources for dealing with depression, but it is my strong conviction that a religious orientation can help here considerably. Of course, the greatest of all losses is the death of a loved one. As we will see, bereavement is a form of reactive depression.

2. *Abstract Losses.* Some losses are not real and tangible. They cannot be seen, weighed, or measured. We call these "abstract" losses. But this does not make them any less powerful as triggers of depression. *Abstract losses* can include such things as the loss of love (as when you are jilted by a lover or a friend leaves town), the loss of self-respect (as when you are criticized by a friend or reprimanded by your boss), the loss of hope or ambition (when your application to graduate school is rejected), or the loss of being needed (when you retire from your employment and/or when your children all finally leave home and start their independent lives).

Some of us experience a loss of power or prestige whenever someone else "equals" us through promotion or through the development of superior skills. These losses may be very abstract, but as far as their ability to trigger depression is concerned, they are equally as powerful as any real loss we may suffer.

In some respects they are more difficult to deal with than real losses as they often are much more elusive and difficult to identify. They affect such vague and unquantifiable needs as security and power, and it takes a lot of careful thought and often professional help to bring these losses into awareness. Unless one identifies the loss, one cannot "work through" the depression. The depression lingers and may even get worse when an abstract loss remains elusive.

3. *Imagined Losses.* Sometimes our imaginations are to blame for our depressions. Imagined losses are neither real nor abstract. In fact, they are not losses at all, but our minds react as if they are. For example, you may find yourself brooding over some incident. Perhaps a neighbor has hinted that your cat is digging up her garden. Your imagination exaggerates the incident and your self-talk expands on what your neighbor has said and you imagine all sorts of rejection.

Perhaps you imagine that you have been snubbed, ridiculed, or rejected (all forms of loss of pride), or you become suspicious that a spouse is betraying you or being unfaithful. Paranoid thoughts like these can be a major cause of imagined losses and depression. Since these losses are only imagined, it is not possible to fully resolve them. The depression of imagined loss is thus very persistent, because no real loss has actually taken place.

The only way you can deal with an imagined loss is to *test its reality*. If you imagine you've been rejected, then test it out. Speak to the one you feel has rejected you. You will either turn it into a real loss (in which case you can now begin to deal with it), or discover there is no loss at all. It may be that some of what you fear has a basis in reality, but most times it is your imagination which has a field day and plays havoc with your emotions. Force yourself to see your imaginations for what they are—imaginations. If necessary, check them out often by asking the right questions or carefully weighing up the odds of their being correct.

4. *Threatened Losses.* Reactive depression can also be caused by a threatened loss. No actual loss may have occurred or need necessarily occur. The threat alone is sufficient to trigger the depression.

As with other types of losses, *threatened losses* can be just as depression-producing as actual losses. Have you ever taken someone who is close to you to the hospital for minor surgery and found yourself somewhat depressed, pacing up and down? You wait patiently with a knot in your stomach, and all need for food is gone. Your head tells you that there is always a risk in any surgical procedure. No actual loss has taken place, but the threat of loss is sufficient to trigger depression.

Life is full of threats. We are threatened by recessions, growing older, the loss of a job, a spouse, a reputation, or some opportunity to make money. These can all cause a reaction of depression just as easily as if an actual loss has occurred.

Often, threatened losses can be most difficult to cope with since they can also play on our imaginations.

Dealing with Depression

Since reactive depression is a response to loss, healing from depression occurs through a process of "griefing." Grief is not only the response to bereavement, it is how we resolve *all* losses. Whether the loss is through death or some other cause, reactive depression facilitates the process of "letting go." If we cooperate with this process we will discover that it holds healing beneath its pain.

To grieve over a loss, one must first identify the loss. Not all losses are what they seem.

1. *List Your Losses.* It can be helpful if you take a moment to prepare a list of those losses you have experienced recently or that you find yourself experiencing repeatedly. Categorize them as real, abstract, imagined, or threatened. Examine your marriage, your job, school life, family life, recreation, goals, and accomplishments, and see how many losses of various types you can identify. Try to recall your last depression experience and identify the underlying loss. This exercise can alert you to repeated experiences of loss and give you some perspective on how you value things, how you set yourself up for unrealistic expectations, and how frequently you distort the severity of a loss. You should discover that life still goes on despite your loss.

2. *Recognize Psychological Factors.* Whether the loss is real, abstract, imagined, or only threatened, psychological factors play an important role in precipitating and perpetuating depression. Obviously, *awareness* of a loss is the first step in a depression reaction. Losses don't affect us while we are asleep. It is only when we become aware of them that we experience the reaction of depression. This is important and gives us an important clue as to how we should handle it. You see, it is not the loss *per se* that causes the depression, but our *interpretation* of the loss. It is what the loss *means* to us in terms of our values, beliefs, and expectations that determines how we will react. This means that if we can get our values sorted out, put our expectations in realistic perspective, and have a right attitude toward life, we can reduce both the frequency and pain of our depressions, shorten their duration, and even avoid them altogether in many cases.

Psychological factors also play an important role in *perpetuating* depression. As we will see shortly, depressions often perpetuate themselves. If what we believe about a loss (and say to ourselves concerning it) triggers a depression, continuing to believe and say these things will perpetuate it. For example, you may have been snubbed by a friend or rejected for some job and experienced a depressive reaction. If you continue to say to yourself, "I am useless," or "I am never going to be able to get a decent job that satisfies me," you will perpetuate the depression and prolong it unnecessarily. You may even intensify the depression and increase your emotional pain.

The Depression Cycle

The ideal way to resolve a depression is to allow yourself to experience the sadness of the loss as deeply as possible. Do your grieving thoroughly. Do not short-circuit the grief process nor oppose the depression in either yourself or anyone else. This will only prolong it.

It is a mistake to say to someone who is depressed, "Come on now, snap out of it. You don't have to be so depressed." We say this because *we* are experiencing discomfort as we observe the other's depression. This advice is callous, ineffective, and often serves only to intensify the depression as it represents further loss because of your implied rejection and criticism.

We must accept that if there has been a legitimate loss, it is *normal* and even *necessary* that the person experiencing the loss grieve over it appropriately. This is as true when the loss is real (as through the death of a spouse) as it is for an abstract or any type of loss. Depression serves a very valuable and protective function in that it helps the sufferer to evaluate and come to terms with the loss. This "ideal" depression cycle is depicted in Figure 4.

Note that the "trigger" of the depression is the awareness and evaluation of the loss—and the depth of the depression will be determined by the significance of the loss. If the cycle is not short-circuited, the person will begin to recover from the depression after a while. Recovery is quite natural if you accept the loss and "let go." Unfortunately, we don't always follow this ideal cycle. What happens more typically is shown in Figure 5.

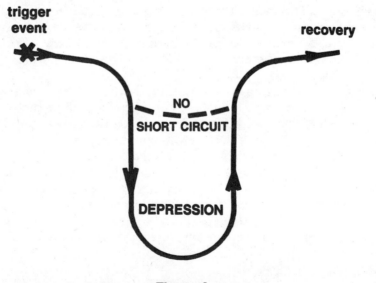

Figure 4

The "Ideal" Depression Response

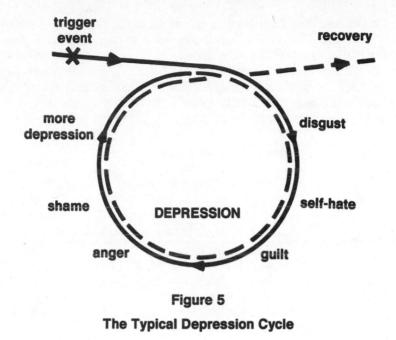

Figure 5
The Typical Depression Cycle

Here, the loss triggers the depression as before, but as soon as the sufferer begins to experience the depression, other reactions are created. The person may react to the feeling of depression with disappointment or even disgust and may even become angry at himself for allowing it to happen. These all represent further losses.

These additional reactions, together with the general state of depression, create feelings of guilt and shame, especially if those around begin to send messages like, "Don't tell me you're depressed again!" or "Come on now, you've·got nothing to be depressed about." Even if these words are not actually verbalized, a sensitive person can "sense" them. In a depressed condition the sufferer can be very tuned in to the body language and attitudes of those around. The end result is a deeper sense of loss to which the person responds with more depression—thus perpetuating the cycle. I call this the "depression cycle," as it can repeat itself over and over again. It will finally lose momentum with the passage of time when feelings ultimately return to normal. Occasionally the intensity of a depression increases and reaches serious proportions. The secondary losses can be very subtle and depend largely for their impact on how accepting we are of our depression, whether others are accepting or condemning of us, and whether we are anger-prone.

This circularity of depression can account for why initial insignificant losses can trigger very deep depressions. The healthiest way to deal with loss is to make sure that you experience an "appropriate" amount of depression. You can overcome the depression more rapidly by avoiding the trap of secondary reactions and not condemning yourself for being depressed. It is enough to cope with the initial loss without creating further losses by fighting the depression.

How to Avoid Perpetuating Depression

The steps to resolving depression are not too difficult to identify and implement. It takes a little discipline at first, but once you have found out how successful the technique is, you will discover that it is a lot less painful to resolve the depression than to go on being depressed. There are six steps.

1. *Recognize Your Depression.* Very often, depression is not recognized for what it is. We may not notice we are depressed until someone else draws attention to it. It can be very helpful to ask someone close to you to tell you whenever they think you are depressed. Don't deny or fight your depression. If you are depressed quite often, you may already have the skill to recognize and admit to your feeling.

Sometimes depression hides behind feelings of extreme fatigue, despondency, lethargy, anger, or plain unhappiness. If you find yourself lacking energy, losing interest in normal activities, feeling that life has no promise, or that you are sad much of the time, you will certainly be experiencing depression. Admit it and label it as such to yourself.

2. *Don't Fight or Resist Depression.* Since reactive depression is a healing emotion and quite natural, it must be allowed to facilitate the grieving process. Resisting it only intensifies secondary reactions and makes you more depressed. Don't blame others for it—force yourself to accept the idea that it is both normal and necessary that you allow yourself to be depressed. The more effective you are in doing this, the more quickly you will recover from the depression.

3. *Identify the Loss That Triggered the Depression.* Ask yourself was it real, abstract, imagined, or threatened? This may be quite easy in some cases but more difficult in others, since the loss may be very subtle and elusive. Talking it over with a friend can help you explore what a certain loss means to you. Examine past experiences that may be similar and see whether you can identify a trend or theme in your reactions. Don't diminish the importance of little things in causing depression. Our emotions don't always respond to logical or rational perceptions, and often very small or innocuous things can trigger

deep feelings of loss. Their power to do this may be caused by earlier life experiences where excessive losses have raised sensitivity to loss.

4. *Face the Reality of the Loss.* If our loss is real, the quicker we can move to accepting the reality of the loss, the better. We have a tendency to deny or avoid facing our losses, creating an irrational hope that the loss will be restored. We are also very selective in receiving information. "I won't believe it. It's just not true!" is a common initial reaction to severe loss, especially bereavement. Such denial only prolongs the pain of depression.

In most cases, facing the reality of a loss inevitably means accepting the irreversibility of it. There are some things in life that cannot be changed. Sometimes you have to force yourself to accept the loss as final as the only way you can go forward and heal your emotion, even though this seems more painful.

If the loss is not real but only imagined, your strategy must be to first check out how real your fears are. You can test the reality of your imagined losses by seeking information that will clarify your fears. If, for example, you imagine that a friend is angry with you and you experience this as a loss, go to the friend and check out your perception. If your friend is really angry, your loss is real and can be dealt with accordingly. If your friend is not angry, you are only wasting your emotional energy by imagining that he is.

In general, the task here is to *convert all your imagined losses to real ones* wherever this can be done. Accept the reality of your real losses and discard the remaining imagined ones. You may be surprised at how many of your imagined fears and losses have no grounds in reality whatsoever. All it takes is a little effort in checking them out.

5. *Develop a Perspective on Your Loss.* We often react to loss as if it were catastrophic. Have you ever received a letter from a friend who is angry at you? Not a pleasant experience! It is easy to exaggerate the rejection. A cloud hangs over you the rest of the day. But then something more serious happens that eclipses the earlier loss. Let's say you have a car accident and injure someone. Now you really feel bad, so much so that the earlier problem seems insignificant. Why? Because the later and more serious problem has altered your perspective on the earlier one. But why does it take a more serious loss to change our perspective? We should be able to restore our perspective *without* waiting for another loss to occur.

The severity of your problems are very much determined by your perspective. If you can develop the ability to put your losses in proper perspective and see them in the context of larger issues, you could speed up your recovery. This "perspective building" can take place at any time, not just when you are depressed. The old-fashioned idea of counting your many blessings whenever faced with tragedy may not be such a bad one after all!

During our early twenties, my wife and I ran a small Sunday school and conducted weekly church services in a run-down area of our city. One day, when I was quite depressed over our financial situation, we visited some of the parishioners. As I recall, the cause of my depression was that I needed a new car but could not afford to buy one. We called on a few homes and finally came to a family where the husband was an alcoholic and had not been home for months. On the morning of our visit, the lady of the house (a mother of three children) had been told by her doctor that she had developed breast cancer. My wife and I counseled and prayed with her as she shared the sad news with us. What do you think happened to my depression? Her catastrophe had restored my perspective. My depression was replaced with much sympathy for this unfortunate lady.

I wondered what she was feeling, so I asked her, expecting to hear her cry of despair. Can you imagine my surprise when she told us that she was thankful to God that the illness had not come earlier in her life? Her children, she said, would have been too young to take care of themselves if this had happened earlier! Now, at least, they were old enough to care for themselves. I could hardly believe my ears. "Thankful to God. . ."

She had put everything in the best perspective she knew and could find something to be thankful for, even in her life-threatening crisis. I learned an important lesson that day: no matter how bad my situation is, it can always be worse. So why not be thankful for the way it is!

We need always to keep our calamities in perspective and have the courage to face them realistically. With God's help we can face and be victorious over *anything* that life has to offer.

6. *Learn from Your Depression.* We can avoid many depressions if we only learn from past experiences of them. Often we will find ourselves repeating the same depression over and over again because we fail to realize that it is the same loss which causes it. Every depression has a lesson to teach us about our values and what we prize in life. If we study our losses we will soon come to see where we need to change.

Take, for example, the losses that unmet expectations can create. You can deal with many unmet expectations by improving your communication. This is especially true in marriage. Make sure that you get agreement ahead of time—or drop your expectations! Since many of your expectations are not going to be satisfied anyway, why hang on to them? If you stop expecting your husband to be a certain way and he surprises you by being what you want him to be, you have a bonus. If he doesn't, nothing is lost. It never ceases to amaze me what an impact unmet expectations can have on relationships. When a couple learns to drop their unnecessary or excessive expectations for each other, they remove the cause of much depression by taking away the ingredients for loss.

I have a sign in my office that says, "*Blessed are they that expect nothing, for they'll not be disappointed.*" At first the sign surprises you, until you get the deeper meaning of it: If you expect too much of others, you will always be disappointed.

Expectations that can be mutually agreed upon and are clearly communicated are obviously permissible; but be prepared to deal with your disappointments when they are not met.

The Christian's Resources for Dealing with Depression

This chapter would not be complete if I did not point out that as Christian believers we have very significant resources for dealing with depression. It is not that life in Christ has no losses. A life of faith does not automatically guarantee that one will never experience loss with the consequent depression. This is as much a part of the Christian's experience as for anyone. It may be harder to accept the depression as a natural reaction, but full reliance on God's resources will bring healing much more quickly. Especially let me stress that it is what we *do* with our depression that determines whether we are living the life of faith or failing to use the provisions that God has given us, not whether or not we are depressed.

What are God's provisions for our healing? There are three important resources that can help us cope with loss and help us do our grieving.

1. *God Gives Perspective for Our Lives.* Knowing God through Christ *must make a difference* in the way we view life and its losses. Living in God provides a vantage point from which we can see the larger plan of God and evaluate our losses and interpret our future in the light of this plan. It forces us constantly to sort out the *essentials* from the *nonessentials* in life. If we can separate the temporal from the eternal and see the larger scope of all God's plan, we should be able to sort out our values and more intelligently interpret our losses. For example, our attitude toward money, possessions, accomplishments, reputations, and our ambitions *must* all be influenced by this perspective. If loss is experienced, it must be filtered through this perspective. If we can say, "This is a nonessential in my life, so

what difference does it make if I lose it?" whenever we experience a disappointment, our losses will be seen to be less. A life lived from God's perspective can change the meaning of much that bothers us.

2. *God Gives Power in Our Lives.* The concept of Christian power has been much undervalued in many Christian circles. We need to rediscover His power in these trying days. I believe that God can come to us in our frailty and weakness and provide us with these extra resources that we need for dealing with life's disappointments. God may not always rescue us from them, but He *always* empowers us to cope with them. He does not leave us to our own meager resources for coping with life. When we seem to reach the end of our own strength and cannot cope anymore, when the burden of the loss we are experiencing is just too heavy for us to carry, we know we can call on God for help. His help is always available. Probably our most common failing is that we wait so long before we call on Him for this power.

3. *Prayer.* Few Christians adequately tap the powerful resource of prayer. They may pray, but most praying doesn't really touch God because it hasn't touched the depths of our own being. We fill our prayers with petty requests which we repeat over and over again.

Prayer is provided for *our* benefit. God does not *need* our prayers in the same sense that we do. When prayer is used honestly and intelligently (and by this I mean that we become absolutely authentic and transparent with God), it cannot leave us unchanged. It is one of the most powerful therapeutic forces I know because it brings all of God's power to bear on our need. There is no psychotherapist more unconditional in accepting you, no psychoanalyst more insightful in understanding your deep motivations, and no cognitive therapist with more clarity of thought and purpose than your Creator. Why not let Him do some therapy with you? Your depression may well be the pain that heals you, if you will let God be a part of it.

Summary

The experience of depression is inevitable in all our lives. While there are biological forms of depression, most of us struggle with reactive depression. Most reactive depressions are a response to a sense of loss, and this loss can be real, abstract, imagined, or only threatened.

Resolving depression involves identifying and accepting the reality of the loss, determining if it is real or abstract, imagined or threatened, testing the reality of imagined or threatened losses, and then allowing yourself to grieve over your loss. You can avoid perpetuating a depression by paying attention to self-talk and being careful about how you react to the depression. By placing your losses in proper perspective, especially the perspective of God's will, you can accept losses more gracefully and avoid much unnecessary depression.

"But what things were gain to me, those I counted loss for Christ. Yea doubtless, and I count all things but loss for the excellency of the knowledge of Christ Jesus my Lord: for whom I have suffered the loss of all things. . ." (Philippians 3:7, 8 KJV).

Additional Reading

1. *Counseling the Depressed,* Archibald D. Hart (Dallas, Texas: Word Books).
2. *Depression and the Body,* Alexander Lowen (New York: Penguin).
3. *The Book of Hope: How Women Can Overcome Depression,* Helen DeRosis and Victoria Y. Pellegrino (New York: Macmillan).
4. Psalm 42 and Philippians 3.

7

Freedom from Self-Hate

"I didn't know who I was, but for the first time I realized I was valuable to somebody."

That's all I heard her say. Yet suddenly I could piece together a complete life story. I could not see her at first because her voice came from in front of me as I stood in line at the bank. Three or four people separated her from me. The words rang once again, loud and clear through my head: " . . . for the first time I realized I was valuable to somebody."

Then I saw her. She was a "little person." Her short arms and legs and large head drew attention to her easily. I guessed her age to be about twenty-five, and while everyone was staring at her, she was quite oblivious to the attention she was generating. The woman she was talking to was tall and attractive, and the conversation quite obviously centered around some recent event in her life.

My mind raced as I tried to piece together her probable life story. I could imagine how resentment had built up within her at the chance misfortune that had created her so small. All her life she had probably drawn attention. From the earliest years of her life she would have felt "different." She saw her friends grow tall while she remained small and awkward, and this must have been very painful for her. I expect that most of the time she would just want to hide away so as not to be in the public's eye. She would fear going into public places and, worst of all, receive those patronizing and humiliating comments that unfeeling people find so easy to let slip.

Then my attention was drawn back to the conversation. She was telling her tall friend how she had become a Christian just six months before. For the first time, she related, she had experienced a wonderful sense of unconditional love and acceptance from God through Christ. Finally in her life she felt she was valuable enough to somebody, and she had now begun to see some value in herself. Her testimony was very clear. Everyone in line heard it. We were all too reserved to shout out a loud "Amen!"

An unusual story? No, I think this is to some extent the life story of us all.

What Is Your Self-Image?

"*Who Am I?*" This is the question that haunts all of us throughout our lives. We are forced to ask this question because within each of us there are features we hate. There are aspects about our personality, looks, voice, and appearance that we dislike a little or a lot, mildly or intensely. We fear that we have not "grown up" in every part of our being, and we begin finding ways early in life to conceal those parts of ourselves we perceive to be inadequate, for fear that when others see them, they will also be repulsed. Like the little person in the bank, we probably all feel that there is something about us that isn't perfect.

What are the features we dislike most? Surprisingly, most people have very personalized inadequacies that center around *two major themes: intelligence and appearance.* One does not have to look for the reasons for this. Our culture clearly worships and prescribes which personal attributes are the most prized. If you are going to succeed in life, you either have to be intelligent or look beautiful or handsome. If you are a man it probably helps to be tall as well! If you have neither the right appearance or intelligence, you are in trouble!

But here is a paradox. While there are many people who are both intelligent and attractive, these qualities are only "relative." There is always someone more intelligent and attractive than you! This leads most of us to feel that we will never match society's standards. There is always someone more intelligent and more attractive than we to steal the limelight. We cannot help but be dissatisfied with who we are. And these feelings of inadequacy continually erode our feelings of self-worth.

Do you remember the story about the children of Israel when they had been delivered out of Egypt and were on their way to the land that God had promised them? As they came near to Cannan, God instructed Moses to send men to spy out the new land. Spies were chosen and duly dispatched with instructions to explore the land and see if it was good or bad. After a while the spies returned, but their reports were conflicting. Some said that what they saw was a land flowing with milk and honey and that although the people were strong, they would be overcome. Other spies had a different story: "And there we saw the giants . . . and we were in our own sight as grasshoppers . . . " (Numbers 13:33 NEB). Giants and grasshoppers! The problem for us is that when we send our "self-evaluation" spies to search the depths of our beings, they come back with the same report: We are only grasshoppers and our enemies are giants. This is the problem of low self-esteem or self-hate—a problem every one of us must struggle with to some extent.

What has Scripture to say about the problem of low self-esteem? The apostle Paul has given us a clear prescription for dealing with our personal "grasshoppers." In psychological language, it is a prescription for developing a healthy self-esteem. While he addresses more directly the problem of *inflated* self-image (too many giants), I believe the principles for dealing with it are the same if the problem is self-hate (too many grasshoppers). Here is what the apostle says: " . . . do not be conceited or think too highly of yourself, but *think* your way to a *sober estimate* based on the measure of faith that God has dealt each of you" (Romans 12:3 NEB [italics added]).

Paul never addresses himself directly to the problem of low self-esteem. The reason for this is obvious: in New Testament times inflated self-esteem (conceit) prevailed. Low self-esteem is a problem more characteristic of our age than his.

Many psychologists feel that an epidemic of inferiority is raging through our society. There are more grasshoppers than giants in the land! In some ways these grasshoppers have always been with us, but what we are experiencing as a phenomenon of twentieth century Western culture is quite unique. It is as if something has gone wrong with our cultural genetics. We can't help perpetuating self-hate in our offspring.

The reasons for this are not hard to find. Our highly industrialized, computerized, and depersonalized society appears to be breeding a mass disillusionment with life and our age. This finds expression in personal rejection—the basis for self-hate. There are very few new frontiers for us to conquer, and only a limited few challenges remain to excite the average person. Most must be content with a humdrum existence, being carried along like a railroad coach in the middle of the train. It doesn't know where it has been nor where it is going. It just follows the rest of the train! With no sense of destiny, no idea of purpose or sense of excitement about life, existence becomes a chore. Is it any wonder that many begin to feel as if they are only grasshoppers? And the rest of life is full of giants—so what hope do they have for conquering their "promised land"?

Self-Image As the Basis for Self-Esteem

Over the last decade there has been an increased focus on self-consciousness. Self-scrutiny has come to be a normal activity, and many schools of psychology encourage this self-focusing. As humans we have the ability to engage in self-reflection. We can literally stand back and observe ourselves. We can study our habits, examine our actions, and review our looks. This forms the basis of "self-image." Out of our evaluation of this self-image we develop a sense of "self-esteem."

This judgment of ourselves depends to a great extent on our values and belief systems. While there is some danger that we might come to overvalue ourselves (we call this conceit), most of us tend to undervalue our images. We call this self-hate or low self-esteem. The chances are much greater that we will develop a preponderance of self-hate. To develop an adequate or healthy self-esteem (note that I don't use the expression "high self-esteem"), it is sufficient to stop hating yourself. For me, a healthy attitude of the self toward the self is the absence of self-hate. I do not encourage the development of exaggerated "self-love." This can easily become narcissism—not a healthy self-attitude.

Closely related to the problem of self-esteem is this idea that one should *love yourself.* You will recall that in response to a scribe who wanted to know which was the first and therefore the most important commandment, Jesus replied, "And thou shalt love the Lord thy God with all thy heart and with all thy soul, and with all thy mind, and with all thy strength . . . " (Mark 12:30 KJV). Almost immediately thereafter He says, "love thy neighbor as thyself" (v. 31). There were no other commandments greater than these. Loving your neighbor "as yourself" has become a very popular notion in Christian circles. It implies that there is a form of self-love or self-valuing that is both appropriate and necessary to relationships with others. Some have even gone so far as to suggest that you cannot love others *unless* you love yourself.

If you are going to be able to value others, you must first be able to see something of value in yourself, they suggest. If you do not love (in the truest sense of the word) and value yourself, you will be unable to value others.

I suppose we understand the intention of such sentiments, but I doubt if they are scriptural.

Some Christian writers have questioned whether "self-love" is biblical. They believe we have misinterpreted Jesus. Did Jesus really mean that we should love our neighbor as ourselves *as a command,* or was He merely in effect saying, "You already love yourself too much; you should therefore love your neighbor just as much"? In other words, the problem boils down to this: Is Jesus presupposing self-love or is He commanding it? Is the focus on the neighbor, or on the self? There is no doubt in my mind that Jesus is addressing Himself *primarily* to the priority of love toward the *neighbor*. He presupposes self-love. He assumes we love ourselves. In fact, the implied criticism is that we love ourselves *too much*. So why not pass some of it on to your neighbor? Read this Scripture again and see if you don't see this meaning.

Paul does the same in Ephesians 5:28 when he tells us to "love our wives as our own bodies." He is not advocating more "body love." He assumes we love our bodies and encourages us to pass the love on to our wives. In neither case is self-love condemned, however, and the difficulty we face in coming to understand how we should feel about ourselves is more a problem with what it means to balance the *love* we should feel toward ourselves and the greater love we must pass on to others.

We intuitively fear self-love because we equate it, quite erroneously, with pride and self-seeking. We cannot see the connection between feeling good about ourselves and yet having a sense of our sinfulness. But this tension is inevitable. Both are true. We are worthy and we are sinful. Adequate self-esteem is a matter of balancing this tension.

Much of our confusion about self-esteem comes from confusing personhood with self-centeredness. Personhood is what makes us who we are. Self-centeredness is an expression of our lower or sinful nature. I may be sinful by nature and selfish by disposition, but this does not mean that my personhood is rotten. It is my deeds, my meager attempts to win God's favor through works, that are as filthy rags in His sight, not the essence of my being. If my personhood was not valuable why would He have died for me?

Furthermore, we should not equate a healthy self-love with self-aggrandizement. To have an adequate self-esteem based on a healthy self-love, it is necessary to have an *accurate self-image*. We must know who and what we are, and no defects must be hidden from our view. Most of us do not have trouble with this. But we must also have enough self-honesty to acknowledge our strengths, our giants. It is so easy to be honest about our grasshoppers, but deny our giants. How else could we use our talents for God?

I believe that a healthy self-esteem is characterized by an *accurate self-appraisal* of *both* strengths and weaknesses—and a willingness to accept one's inadequacies. This is a healthy self-love. It is not based on an exaggerated sense of personal strengths. It is consistent with the recognition of our basic sinfulness and a willingness to receive God's grace.

It is at this point that the Christian gospel provides us with a clear answer to the problem of low self-esteem. Without God we are left to struggle with our flaws and inadequacies, to scrape together from our failures and imperfections some semblance of self-respect. By engaging in massive denial and rejection of the opinions of others, we can at best build a "pseudo" healthy self-esteem. Its superstructure is flimsy. It is based on self-distortion—a fragile support for self-confidence. The facade of this "pseudo" self-esteem is merely a camouflage for the many grasshoppers that pervade our being and maintain our self-hate.

The Consequences of Low Self-Esteem

The consequences of self-hate are far-reaching. Its influence is like a cancer, both in the individual and society. Low self-esteem breeds depression and anger. It robs us of vitality and confidence. Many who lack adequate assertiveness do so because they do not feel valuable enough to present their claims and assert their rights. Self-hate breeds judgmentalism and criticism and affects our interpersonal relationships in many ways. It permeates every aspect of our lives. And Christians do not escape the destruction that self-hate causes.

Perhaps the most unfortunate consequence of self-hate is that it creates phony facades. To make up for our perceived short-comings, we hide behind false faces and feel like hypocrites. As we go through childhood we learn ways to defend ourselves against perceived personal weaknesses. Since we don't want to be hurt by the rejection of others, we withdraw and build shells of self-concealment. These phony facades are of two types. In one we set about magnifying our giants, using, of course, selective attention and exaggeration. We distort our self-image by ignoring or even denying our real strengths, focusing on inadequacies and refusing to display our strong points. We fear failure and go to ridiculous extremes to conceal our short-comings.

For some there is the risk of developing an inflated sense of worthiness. You may devote all your energy to hiding your grasshoppers and to displaying your giants. You take pride in little accomplishments and show off your minor successes. You must look perfect at all costs and become supersensitive to criticism or failure. You rush to plug up every crack in your concealment lest a trickle of criticism becomes a flood of truth about yourself that could shatter the fragile self-confidence you have built. This is conceit, and it is a false strength.

The other type of phony facade is one in which we exaggerate our grasshoppers, or the "little strengths" we see in ourselves. We become totally preoccupied with our inadequacies and spend all our energy trying to change them. We hate ourselves for what we are and soon come to hate everyone else also. Becoming too self-critical and self-rejecting, we almost welcome failure because it proves we are no good, and we use it as self-punishment. We lack sufficient confidence to make progress and become paranoid about how we are perceived. We prefer staying away from people rather than risk displaying our weaknesses. We fear that people won't like our grasshoppers. Feeling that we have nothing of any worth to offer, we pull back and don't risk new friendships or new endeavors.

Both these phony facades place us in a perpetual bind. The reactions of others are not to our true selves but to our facades. However, by some mental juggling we actually *expect* people to respond to our true selves. So, whenever we get a compliment or word of approval, it counts for little. We never know whether people are responding to our masks or to our true selves.

Conversely, whenever we are criticized it hurts more than it should and is seldom constructive. This confusion places us in a bind. We can never grow under these conditions. The seeds of psychological growth (social interaction with others) fall on the stony ground of our confusion and disbelief, preventing us from developing a realistic image of our true selves. And we need a realistic image to be the foundation for self-esteem. To have a realistic self-image we must be open to honest feedback to our true selves from those we can trust. Without this feedback our self-image remains distorted and our self-esteem continues as self-hate.

The Causes of Low Self-Esteem

Psychological theories differ greatly in the centrality of the problem of low self-esteem and in identifying its causes. Generally, there are only two points of agreement: 1) the foundation for self-esteem (high or low) is laid early in life; 2) interpersonal relationships play a major role in its development.

The main causes of high or low self-esteem are found in our early childhood and arise largely from how we relate to significant people in our lives. The members of our family are the major source of early self-esteem. This places a tremendous responsibility on those of us who are parents or grandparents. Unfortunately, if either or both parents suffer from a problem of low self-esteem, this is easily transmitted to their children. Many psychological studies support the commonly held view that positive and loving acceptance of the child by its parents is correlated with the development of high self-esteem. However, if a parent is not self-accepting, or is abusive and overly critical, it will be difficult for that child to develop a positive self-image.

Parents often live out their unfilled ambitions through their children. By so doing they make excessive demands on their offspring. If a child fails, a parent may become critical and condemn the child excessively, because he is projecting his own failure onto the situation. This condemnation then builds a feeling of inadequacy and unworthiness in the child.

The most powerful force we have for controlling our children is love. When our children are very young, we love them unconditionally. They may aggravate or anger us, but we go on loving them anyway. As they get older, we begin to punish them by withdrawing our love whenever they displease us. Our love gradually becomes conditional.

Not only do we reject when we withdraw our love, but we may even verbalize our rejections and use labels like "dumb" or "stupid." Slowly the child begins to internalize these labels and the implied rejection and starts labeling himself or herself as "good" or "bad." The effect of this is devastating, especially during the critical years of early childhood. It *always* builds self-hate and low self-esteem.

There is abundant research to show that a high level of self-esteem in the parents produces a more consistent atmosphere of unconditional love and acceptance. This optimizes the development of high self-esteem in children. Low self-esteem in the parents, even when it is concealed behind a super-spiritual mask and covered by lots of church activity, seldom begets high self-esteem in children.

Closely related to the parents' self-esteem and their treatment of their children as a cause of low self-esteem, are the values and expectations which parents unwittingly impose on their children. Certain societal values are more highly prized by some parents than others and may cause children to set up an internal system of self-rejection and self-punishment.

For example, our society prizes physical appearance. Through television and movies we worship and present as the "standard" a certain type of physique and facial features which we equate with beauty or handsomeness. In so doing we communicate to our children (and perpetuate from generation to generation) the idea that unless they match these standards they will never make it. As the father of three daughters I know at first hand the pain of watching a child come to terms with her appearance and how it matches our world's standards. Nearly every adolescent I have ever had in therapy has had some problem with self-rejection as it relates to physical appearance. It is always a major concern affecting their self-esteem. As babies they were admired and adored. In the early years of life they were repeatedly told that they were perfectly beautiful. Then the day came when they faced reality. Every child must eventually discover that he or she is either too fat or too thin, too tall or too short. The sudden (or gradual) realization that imperfections are many and far removed from the ideals portrayed in the media, will come as a bitter disappointment to most of us.

The saddest aspect of this is that these values are absolutely culturally dependent. The same physique or facial characteristics that are rejected in one culture may be highly prized in another. It is all a matter of genetics and the luck of the draw as to whether you are born into a culture that prizes your given physique.

As parents we easily and unwarily buy into this system of values in many subtle ways. We give little thought to the emotional harm our values can create. In many subtle ways we send the message that appearance is everything. By careful thought and adjustment to our thinking, we can change this message. Beauty is what exists inside, not outside.

I am not advocating that we should never correct our physical imperfections. Plastic surgeons, orthodontists, and tailors can work wonders for many of us. But where do we draw the line? Eventually we will find that there are imperfections that cannot be corrected. There is only one thing we can then do—find the freedom of self-acceptance. Be content to just be yourself.

But our society does not only prize appearance. It also prizes performance. Those who feel inadequate in appearance can always try to make it with some intellectual achievement or success in a special endeavor. Get straight A's, and this compensates for what you look like! Excel in sports, and the girls will worship you whatever you look like! We start pushing our children from an early age to compensate in this way. Perform, perform, perform!

Of course, if you have both appearance and performance, you are a hero and will be worshiped. But since we cannot all succeed in compensating for nature's oversights and we certainly can't choose our genes, some of us must fail to make it and will end up feeling bad about ourselves and believing that we are of no value to anybody. What can such a person do?

A Christian Approach to Self-Esteem

A common approach in Christian psychological circles is to see God's love and acceptance of us as the underlying dynamic for correcting low self-esteem. To experience unconditional love from God through His grace is to experience the basis for a healthy self-concept. This idea is unique to Christianity. There is nothing you do to earn favor with God. Appearance and performance count for nothing. We come to accept God's love for us and this transforms our love for ourselves. No doubt the acceptance of this idea at a very deep level can transform a person's life and provide a new sense of being valued by somebody else. This was the experience of the "little person" I mentioned at the start of this chapter. You cannot remain unmoved by God's love. If you really believe that God loves you unconditionally, you must begin to value yourself. It must bring a revolutionary change to your life, particularly to your self-esteem. But this deals with only one part of the problem. Many have experienced this love from God—but go on hating themselves!

For the little person I encountered in the bank, it was revolutionary to find in God the first unconditional love and acceptance she had ever experienced. She was now valued and could begin to value herself. The problem is that this experience of being greatly valued by God comes at a stage in most of our lives when it is difficult for it to undo the patterns established over many years. The problem of our low self-esteem lies deeply rooted in our psyches. The foundation was laid for self-distortion and self-rejection at a very early age so that it may take some time and a process of assimilation to change this foundation.

This is not to say that the Spirit of God cannot eradicate these roots and correct the faulty foundations of self-hate right at salvation. I have personally witnessed many such apparently miraculous transformations. But most of the Christians I have counseled have found it to be a much slower process of growth. Partly this is due to their inability to really believe God and utilize His provisions. Partly it is due to the nature of the problem and that God deals with such issues through a process of sanctification. Unfortunately, many new Christians are led to believe that personality problems can be cured instantly. This is not so! Most Christian psychotherapists I know are often confronted by disillusioned and disappointed new Christians who cannot understand why all their problems have not been instantly removed. While some aspects of Christian development may take place instantly, much is the result of process and growth. This is especially true in the area of self-hate. God must work retroactively as well as proactively. This requires a constant attitude of commitment and willingness to change on your part.

To deal with low self-esteem (as with many other emotional problems), it is necessary to reconstruct some aspects of the early part of your life. Those of you who have lived the Christian life for many years will know that while some growth steps seem to be revolutionary and instantaneous, most of the process is just plain hard work. Nowhere does the New Testament lead us to believe that from the moment of our commitment to God we will no longer have any problems or any need to repair past damage and inadequacies. "Think your way," Paul says, "to a sober estimate of yourself" (Romans 12:3 NEB). Thinking means work. Sanctification takes blood and tears. God's refining fire is often hot and uncomfortable. But this is how He works to purify His people.

To repair low self-esteem we need to do an effective job of reconstructing our self-attitudes. For some of us, Christian commitment may put us at greater risk for lowering self-esteem. We can easily set ourselves up to fear and avoid failure. We may set our ideals too high and develop a heightened awareness of our sinfulness and of our moral obligations. Every personal failure is then exaggerated because it implies that our life in Christ is not perfect. We easily increase our self-hate and self-rejection if we are not on guard against these ideas.

Calling Out Your Grasshoppers

Let us now look more closely at Paul's prescription for repairing a distorted self-image as presented in Romans 12:1–3. There are three important steps. These are consistent with a Christian view of personhood. The steps are:

1. the acceptance of God's unconditional love,
2. the development of realistic self-knowledge, and
3. complete self-acceptance.

All those steps are essential to a healthy self-esteem.

1. God's Unconditional Love

As I have already indicated, the first of these steps is foundational. Any effort to establish a sense of self-worth from within one's own being is a lost cause. By far the majority of us are doomed to apparent failure by our appearance, our conversation, our behavior, and our lack of achievements. We cannot rely on them for self-worth. At best, each of us can erect a very flimsy facade and a phony self-image. Our basic worth must be founded outside of our human potential (or lack of it). God in His redemptive work on the cross and His subsequent call to all men to receive His salvation provides the essential basis for our self-worth. Becoming a "new creation" in Christ and finding that we are acceptable to God Himself *must* revolutionize our view of ourselves. Only then do we have the courage and power to call out and deal with our grasshoppers. No longer need we fear the ultimate of all rejections. God has promised Himself to us.

2. The Development of Realistic Self-Knowledge

Paul clearly outlines this as the next step: "*Think* your way to a *sober* estimate" (see Romans 12:3 NEB). A "sober" estimate of yourself is an honest and realistic estimate. Realistic self-knowledge is an essential part of healthy self-esteem. Any distortion of your self-understanding will produce a distorted self-image. If acceptance of yourself as a worthwhile being is based on the effective concealment and avoidance of your shortcomings (so that you are no longer aware of them), you cannot have a healthy self-esteem. Every time a grasshopper raises its head, you are going to be threatened. You must develop a realistic awareness of who and what you are, no matter how painful this may be. This is where pride differs from a high or healthy self-esteem. Many Christians fear that if they feel good about themselves they may be committing the sin of pride. But pride is characterized by *unrealistic* self-knowledge. It is self-concealment, not self-knowledge. This form of pride is usually associated with an inflated self-image which is trying to compensate for feelings of inferiority. It is a mechanism of defense which has been erected against feelings of inferiority. We may take "pride" in our accomplishments when we feel insecure and do not have a realistic understanding of our true strengths.

We resort to pride when we need to exaggerate our few giants in order to overcome the threat of our grasshoppers. It is quite different from having a healthy self-esteem, because the latter is based on *realistic* self-knowledge. Humility is the opposite of pride.

The development of realistic self-knowledge in someone with low self-esteem invariably demands that many distortions be corrected. It is common to find persons whose image of themselves was formed early in their lives but continues to dominate now. It may bear no relation to who they are now. Mostly we are not as bad as we have come to believe we are. Our grasshoppers are *not* as small and as many as we fear, and over the years we have probably concealed or deliberately ignored our giants. Generally, we tend to exaggerate our failings and minimize our strengths. This distortion robs us of a healthy self-esteem.

It can be a most rewarding experience to take someone through the process of realistically evaluating these distortions and correcting them. To watch someone discover his or her true self is one of the great joys of being a therapist.

To facilitate this discovery you should share the process with someone else. While I know of those who have, in the privacy of their prayer life, been able to successfully perform this task, God has created us to be in a fellowship relationship with others. A close friend (or a small group) who can be trusted can help considerably. Begin by listing all the "grasshoppers" or weaknesses you can identify in your life. Alongside set down your giants. Then go over these with a close friend, carefully evaluating each one and adding or subtracting to the list according to your friend's advice. Do not minimize or deny your shortcomings, and don't resist acknowledging your strengths. Your goal is to develop *realistic* self-knowledge and to get a clear picture of yourself. Be honest. Have the courage to face your imperfections. Ask your friend to be genuine and yet not deliberately critical. Take it slowly and don't rush the process. In return you can do the same for your friend—in fact, it would be more effective if it were a mutually shared process.

Having prepared this list of strengths and weaknesses and having obtained agreement on it from your friend, examine each of your "grasshoppers" or weaknesses first. Ask yourself, "Is this really a weakness?" Accept that there are parts of your personality that have never been allowed to grow up or mature. With some effort and encouragement you might be able to transform these grasshoppers into giants, from liabilities into assets.

We all have some underdeveloped areas in our lives. We can love better. We can be more transparent with others. We can be more dependable. Plan a way for turning these weaknesses into strengths. Often all it takes is a change in the way you view your liabilities. Believing that they can be improved is enough to begin the improvement.

You should also take a hard look at your giants. Perhaps you have never allowed yourself to own and value them. Talents are to be developed and used, not hidden away. In some strange manner, whenever there are too many grasshoppers around, our giants tend to lose their power and go into hiding. A right attitude toward your strong points should help you to develop more courage to accept your weaknesses. Ask God to show you how you can use your strengths and then dedicate them to Him to be used in His service.

Remember that this process is a dynamic one; you should not expect it to be completed at any one sitting. When you first start, you may find yourself dealing only with very obvious and superficial aspects of your personality. As you work through these, you will find yourself discovering more subtle and elusive grasshoppers and identifying giants you did not know existed. Keep it up and repeat the process at various stages in your life. You will always find something to work on.

3. Complete Self-Acceptance

The third step is to come to the place of complete self-acceptance. It is the most difficult step, mainly because it involves dealing with much irrationality in your thoughts and beliefs. You may find it easier to identify your strengths and weaknesses, especially if you have the help of an insightful and honest friend, than accept them. But the step of complete self-acceptance is essential and can only be taken by yourself.

Why is this step necessary? Thinking one's way through to "a sober estimate" involves more than just giving intellectual assent to a set of positive and negative qualities about oneself. There may be some weaknesses you will be able to change if you are sufficiently motivated and know how to use the resources available to you. These changes can be accomplished (or at least the process commenced) without much difficulty. But what are you going to do about those aspects of your person you don't like and cannot change? Become despairing? I hope not. Continue your self-hate? Absolutely not. This will only cause you to become more resentful. The more you know about yourself, the greater will be your resentfulness if you cannot accept what you know. Whether it is something that is fixed and unchangeable or something that can be changed, you must begin at the same point: *Complete Self-Acceptance.*

In asking you to take this step, I am not advocating that you resign yourself to your inadequacies. You need to work at changing whatever can be changed. This is simply a step in which you realistically recognize where you are now. It is a starting point. It frees you from the shackles of self-condemnation and avoids the trap of not knowing what to do with what you cannot change. You must move yourself to the place of acceptance without resentment of what you cannot change, knowing where you stand on those aspects that can be altered. This takes courage. And this is where Christ can make the difference in your life. It is on the basis of what He has done for you that you can accept yourself just as you are.

A friend of mine taught me this lesson so forcibly about twenty years ago that I have never forgotten it. He was a graduate of Fuller Seminary and had gone to Africa to do mission work. He was a charming man, loved by everyone who met him. But he hadn't always been this way. In his earlier life he had hated one of his grasshoppers: *He hated his nose.* He saw it as long and protruding and despised it. Consequently, he had begun to despise his whole being. One day, by himself, he came to terms with his flaw. He had realistic self-knowledge—it stared at him out of the mirror every day. But he had never taken the step of total self-acceptance. I suppose plastic surgery could have changed his nose, but this would not be self-acceptance. On his knees before God, he prayed for self-acceptance—and a wonderful sense of freedom followed. As he sat there looking at his flaw, he was able to say to himself, "It's O.K." From that day forward he was a different man. "Here, world, you better take me as I am, because this is all I have to offer," became his favorite expression. With it came a new attitude and a freedom that made him a beautiful person. Everyone liked him. No one even noticed his nose! He had the courage to accept himself unconditionally and set himself free.

But this step must also include making room for failure. We fear failure more than we care to admit, and since we are only human it is inevitable that failure will one day come our way. The development of realistic self-knowledge should therefore include an honest appraisal of our failure proneness and a review of our attitude toward failure. Self-acceptance must include giving ourselves permission to fail, so that failure, when it comes, will not devastate our self-image.

All this can be obstructed by irrational thought processes. As humans we have a tremendous capacity for irrational thinking. Feelings of inadequacy and inferiority can often be based on unrealistic expectations for oneself—which in turn can lead to irrational beliefs of low self-worth. For example, the unrealistic expectation that one must succeed *at all times and in everything* is a common one. Ridiculous? Of course, it is, when stated as bluntly as this. But most of us behave as if it were absolutely true. Check yourself out the next time you fail at something. How much allowance do you make for failing? If you fail once in one hundred times, do you give yourself a high score or a low score? No matter how many times you have succeeded, my guess is that the first time you fail you cancel all your successes and come down hard on yourself for this one failure.

"Failures are to grow by," a friend once said to me. How right he was. Then why do we use failures for self-destruction and not for growing? God does not demand that we succeed at everything we do—we place this demand on ourselves. In any event, most of our failures are of our own creation. We prepare ourselves for failure by setting unrealistic goals and then expecting that we must meet them without any provision for a miss.

I know a housewife, for example, who is criticized by her husband whenever she attempts some new recipe. Never has he complimented her when she tries something new. This upsets her terribly and causes many conflicts. Doe she stop and consider that she may have cooked nine perfect meals in a row and this is the first failure out of ten attempts? No, she is devastated over one criticism. Instead of saying to herself, "It is unfortunate that I can only succeed nine times out of ten," she says, "I have failed this once, therefore I am a bad cook." She may not be able to do anything about her husband's criticism, but she can certainly do a lot about how she interprets his criticism.

Unrealistic expectations and beliefs like these need to be challenged constantly in order to eradicate self-hate. When stated in their extremes, their ridiculous nature becomes apparent. They are unfounded, do not have enough evidence to substantiate them, and need to be discarded as quickly as possible.

Our gospel is amazingly free of these irrational expectations. First, we are accepted for what we are. Second, provision is made for dealing with our failures and inadequacies. Third, we do not have to depend entirely on ourselves. In fact, we are expected to rely on the resources outside of ourselves to accomplish our "perfecting." The irrationality of a lot of what we see in our Christian communities is of our own creation. The gospel is inherently "healthy" and should create in its followers those who are sound in mind as well as in spirit. If it fails to do this, it is because we have not utilized the resources available to us.

Summary

Low self-esteem is caused by self-hate. Our culture sets us up to experience our inadequacies in such a way that we readily develop a distorted image of ourselves. Overvaluing of appearance and performance leaves many feeling inadequate. While Paul's prescription in Romans 12:3 mainly addresses the problem of inflated self-esteem or conceit, the principles for remedying low self-esteem or self-hate are the same:

- Accept God's unconditional love.
- Develop realistic self-knowledge.
- Accept yourself unconditionally.

While the acceptance of God's unconditional love is foundational to a healthy self-esteem, active steps need to be taken to achieve a realistic self-image and total and unconditional self-acceptance. Irrational expectations and erroneous ideas about failure must be dealt with if a healthy self-esteem is to be maintained.

Additional Reading

1. *Healing Grace,* David A. Seamands (Wheaton, Illinois: Victor Books).
2. *Self Talk: Key to Personal Growth,* David Stoop (Old Tappan, New Jersey: Power Books).
3. *Hide and Seek,* James Dobson (Old Tappan, New Jersey: Fleming H. Revell).
4. Mark 12:28–34.
5. Romans 12:1–5.

8

Freedom from Guilt

Guilt is all around us. Everyone experiences some degree of guilt. We feel guilty about our children, our parents, our jobs, even our pets—just everything. It is hard to escape from it. Not all this guilt is neurotic or bad. Some guilt is essential. It keeps us fulfilling our obligations and acting as responsible members of society. Our credit system depends on it! We pay our debts because of guilt; we often love because of guilt; and—saddest of all—sometimes we even love God only out of guilt!

Of all the emotions, guilt must be the one with the most overlap between psychology and theology. Theologians, philosophers, and psychologists have talked about guilt since the dawn of their respective disciplines, and all have tried to find in its understanding the key to spiritual, mental, and emotional health. Unfortunately, though, when theologians talk about guilt they mainly don't mean quite the same thing as when psychologists talk about it. This can be very confusing to the lay person, since what they mainly experience is the guilt psychologists talk about. So right at the outset let me explain the main difference. Psychological guilt is a "feeling" or emotion. Spiritual or theological guilt is a "state of being." We can be spiritually guilty, yet not "feel" anything. We can feel guilty, but not be in a state of guilt. Confusing? Perhaps, but read on!

The difference between that form of guilt which is entirely "psychological" and that which is "theological" is quite considerable. If you confuse the two, you can make yourself vulnerable to increased psychological guilt. Believing you are spiritually guilty can create a lot of guilt feelings.

It is important, therefore, that we make clear the distinction between psychological and spiritual guilt. Emotional and spiritual healthiness depends largely on how effectively we deal with both. The distinction between the two will become clear as we proceed.

While much psychological guilt has no spiritual component, being caused by our early upbringing and training, I do believe that

God has made provision for us to deal with both forms. It is precisely here that we cannot escape the inevitable close relationship between spiritual and psychological aspects of our being. The purpose of this chapter, therefore, will be to deal primarily with our *psychological* guilt, but in the context of our spiritual or theological guilt.

Christians Are Not Exempt from Guilt Problems

A young man once consulted me about a problem he considered to be serious. I was his last desperate hope for help! He had been counseled by many ministers and evangelists without any relief; his problem only became worse after each encounter. Four years previously he had become a Christian by responding to an altar call at an evangelistic meeting. He had made some progress in his faith since then and had offered himself as a candidate for the Christian ministry. The problem, as he described it to me, was that whenever he attended an evangelistic meeting and an altar call was given, he felt an overwhelming compulsion to respond to the invitation and go forward. He could not resist the urge. He could not understand why he should feel this "compulsion," as he was secure in his basic commitment. It was not a spiritual but a psychological issue, he felt.

Needless to say, whenever he counseled with a minister about his problems, he was told that he had to take the urge seriously, since it could be that God was speaking to him. It happened so often that he had become very despondent. He now feared going to church and was becoming a recluse.

As we explored the problem together, it became obvious to me that his problem was indeed one of psychological guilt. Early in his life he was subjected to strong pressure from his parents to conform to their beliefs. As a small child he had been forced to "go forward" often. This had conditioned him to feel guilty every time a call to repentance was made.

Over the weeks following I explained how psychological guilt worked and expanded more fully for him the real meaning of God's forgiveness. Slowly his emotional pain lifted. His Christian commitment also began to take on new meaning and depth.

As believers we are not exempt from the psychological influences of neurotic or unhealthy guilt. Unless we learn how to tell the one type from the other we will always be handicapped in our growth toward spiritual and psychological health. We will feel guilty when we shouldn't, and not feel guilty when we should. This confusion is of our own creating, and what lies behind it is a faulty understanding of the nature of grace and forgiveness.

Unresolved Guilt

Frequently I encounter Christian believers who have not resolved their guilt proneness. They continue to experience exaggerated guilt. This is puzzling to them because they try hard to believe in God's forgiveness. Becoming a Christian does not automatically correct psychological guilt problems. It is the application of the resources of the gospel that brings healing.

It is true that "spiritual" guilt can trigger a valid state of "psychological" guilt. When you become aware of how you stand before God it is quite natural that you "feel" guilty. However, spiritual guilt does not have the same irrational quality that psychological guilt has. It is more constructive, reparative, and amenable to forgiveness. Psychological guilt can easily become neurotic guilt.

For example, let us suppose that one has perfectionist tendencies. By "perfectionist" here, I mean someone who makes impossible, unrealistic demands on herself or himself. We all have perfectionistic *traits*. We tidy up behind others and dislike dirty dishes left in the sink. We can't stand to see anything dirty or disorganized. These traits are not necessarily unhealthy. True perfectionists, however, have a built-in system of self-punishment which is invoked whenever they feel that they are not measuring up to the standards of performance they have set for themselves. Such people may feel that they must be out of bed by at least 6:00 A.M. If for some reason they oversleep, they punish themselves throughout the day by being self-critical or depressed. They feel guilty for having violated their arbitrary 6 A.M. rising rule. If, in addition, they believe that God wants them to be out of bed by that hour, they could easily interpret their feelings of guilt as God's conviction. Psychological guilt is thus transformed to spiritual guilt. Such guiltiness does not easily respond to forgiveness. The two forms of guilt are intermingled and demand punishment as the only way of obtaining relief.

It is possible, of course, for ministers and evangelists unwittingly to utilize psychological guilt mechanisms for creating a state of spiritual guilt. Much modern evangelism makes this mistake with very damaging consequences. This misuse has long been the cause of much concern as it gives rise to spurious conversions and commitments which, in turn, hamper further spiritual development. It becomes harder and harder for the victims of this mixing of guilts to fully appropriate the forgiveness of God.

I have seen this abuse carried so far that it caused a number of suicides in one church. The pastor unwittingly created very intense psychological guilt in a group of young people, and they became so depressed that some of them took their own lives. Whether or not God can turn such abuse into something good is difficult for me to decide. I doubt, however, if in the long run this misuse produces meaningful conversions. We do not need psychological tricks to bring people to Christ. It is unnecessary and may even be detrimental.

The Central Role of Guilt in the Neuroses

I have already alluded to the connection between psychological guilt and the neuroses. Again and again psychologists and psychiatrists have returned to placing guilt at the heart of the neuroses. David Hume, the eighteenth-century Scottish philosopher, claimed that guilt was fundamental to every problem in human personality. Karen Horney contends that guilt feelings play a central role in neurosis. By this she does not mean that all neurotics are immoral, but merely that they feel more guilt.

The role of guilt was also central to Sigmund Freud, the founder of psychoanalysis. He strongly contended for the centrality of guilt. Rollo May, a contemporary psychologist who was first a minister before becoming a psychologist, takes an existential approach and sees neurotic guilt as the end product of unconfronted, unresolved, normal guilt. He also claims that normal guilt is both necessary and healthy, an important point that is frequently overlooked. And so I could go on and on. There is hardly a prominent psychological theorist who does not give a seat of prominence to the problem of guilt.

For me, the most significant thing about guilt is that it frequently triggers other emotional reactions or is triggered by them. It is probably the most common "chained emotion." If I get angry at my child and shout at him, I will almost immediately begin to experience a feeling of guilt. "You should never shout or lose your temper," my mother taught me. So when I do, I feel guilty. We feel sorrow for what we have done and then try to reduce our guilt. The result is a large swing from one set of emotions (shouting and anger) to another set (placating and reconciling). All very unsettling to our children.

Or we might become depressed by something. As soon as we are aware of our depression we feel guilty and react with further depression because we don't like being depressed. Guilt, therefore, can play havoc with our emotions. It is a major cause of neurosis.

Guilt and Anger

Guilt triggers anger very easily, because anger is a way of fighting guilt. I might come home from work, having forgotten to stop and buy something my wife has asked me to get. As I walk in the front door and see my wife, I remember her request. I begin to feel guilty for not complying. But rather than admit my guilt I react by getting angry. "You always ask me to get something for you when you know I'm busy. I've got more important things to think about." By attacking her, I attempt to alleviate my guilt feelings and at the same time prevent her from attacking me for my forgetfulness.

Many a wife has been trapped by that helpless look on her husband's face as he peers into his sock drawer and finds it empty. "You should have told me you were near the end of your socks," she protests in anger. "You knew very well that mother was coming to visit and that I don't have time to do the wash."

Why does guilt sometimes trigger anger? Because guilt is a warning—a signal that something has been violated. It creates an internal tension and a threat of rejection. Anger is one way of fighting this rejection.

Where Does Guilt Come From?

Most people believe that guilt is produced by something we call a "conscience." But what is conscience? Does it exist in a special part of the brain? Are we born with it, or do we learn it? These questions are not as easy to answer as you might expect.

Philosophers have tended to see conscience as a form of moral consciousness—a sense of what is right or wrong—without being too concerned about where it comes from. Theologians have tended to emphasize that it is "the rule of divine power expressing itself in a person's judgments." But is all conscience shaped by God? I don't think so. Generally, psychologists see conscience as an expression of values that have been acquired from parents and teachers and become internalized as part of the personality.

For our purposes we need not be too concerned about technical correctness. There may or may not be a "conscience center" in the brain. I happen to believe that conscience is a function of the whole mind, not any center. It is sufficient for us to recognize that we have a God-given capacity to know right from wrong and to feel good or bad about this knowledge. Feeling good or feeling bad is part of our conscience. Psychologists and theologians owe a great debt of gratitude to Freud, the founder of psychoanalysis, for emphasizing that the activity of conscience goes on without our awareness. Freud also recognized two forms of conscience—one positive and one negative. The "ideal" or positive aspect pushes us to strive for or be attracted to that which we see as good. The prohibitive or negative aspect condemns us for what is bad. The negative aspects of guilt are the first to develop, whereas the positive aspects come later. The state of tension (a state of anxiety) we feel whenever we evaluate something as wrong is what we call "guilt."

How do we learn *what* to feel guilty about? Do's and don'ts come mainly from our parents, and most of it is learned very early in life. To simplify the explanation the process goes something like this: When we first enter the world we are loved unconditionally. Fortunately, we are loved for what we are, not for what we do. We are the pride and joy of our parents, and even though we may be an inconvenience and cause some extra work, we are generally appreciated and accepted. As we begin to come into awareness of our world, however, our parents begin to replace their unconditional love with love that is conditional. We are loved when we do the right thing, but not loved (and perhaps even rejected) when we do wrong. The withdrawal of parental love is partly caused by the anger and frustration they feel at our not doing what they want us to. Slowly, as we continue to grow, we internalize the conflict between being accepted and being rejected. We begin to condemn ourselves without waiting for parental condemnation.

There are, of course, other factors that influence the development of our guilt, but mainly it is a process of internalizing the controls of our parents. Sometimes our parents may even add a little flavor to the process by throwing in a few words like "You are dumb, aren't you?" Or, "You are stupid, bad, and disgusting!" We can also internalize these symbols of rejection and create a sense of shame. Needless to say, our self-esteem suffers as a by-product of this guilt induction. So a severe conscience and low self-esteem often go together.

Not surprisingly, physical discipline, properly and appropriately administered, produces a much healthier internalized conscience than the verbal discipline most often employed by parents. Verbal discipline (shouting, calling the child names) is used mainly because it is easier to administer. You can shout across the room to reprimand a child without getting out of your chair. It may be convenient for you, but it is damaging to the child.

Physical discipline does not necessarily have to involve hitting or spanking. It can include a variety of techniques such as loss of privileges, time spent away from toys, not watching TV, or not visiting friends. Moderate and appropriate physical discipline is not as damaging as might be expected. It is less likely to cause guilt problems later in life because the penalty for the misdeed is paid immediately. It is over and done with. Verbal discipline, and especially the withholding of love, can prolong punishment. Verbal methods can also be more cruel than physical (except in cases of child abuse). Think back to your own childhood. The chances are that you remember the verbal cruelties (things your father called you) more painfully than physical (provided the latter was not excessively cruel).

Not only do we use love and approval to train our children's consciences, we also use them to manipulate and hurt back. We force our children to ask for forgiveness whenever they have wronged us, or we create strong feelings of guilt because they don't love us enough or because they get angry. This manipulation is deeply embedded in the personality of the child and may last throughout life, as many can no doubt attest. I know a seventy-year-old man who still responds to situations as if his mother were hovering over him!

Two Forms of Conscience

It is also helpful to understand that there is not just one conscience. In fact, there may be many. I will focus on two forms, merely to illustrate this point. Can you let your conscience be your guide? Not always. It depends on which conscience. You may be on shaky ground if you depend too much on only one of your consciences to guide your behavior. Conscience is usually helpful, but since it can be so easily distorted and is merely a reflection of an internalized set of values which have been *learned* we need to be cautious. The conscience can easily be distorted.

Conscience can also be warped in other ways. It can be "underdeveloped" and inadequate to guide us because it lacks any sensitivity, or it can be "overdeveloped." It all depends on the atmosphere of your upbringing.

Conscience can be a problem in both extremes. If it is overdeveloped and dominates your personality, you may find yourself imprisoned. You will impose moral standards on yourself more out of the fear of consequences than because of any genuine concern for morality. You will feel guilty almost all the time about everything you do. It becomes impossible to assert yourself and stand up for very basic rights without feeling guilty. You cannot say "no" to a request and have great difficulty confronting someone who is hurting you. This guilt problem, therefore, impacts many areas of your life.

On the other hand, it is possible to suffer from an inadequately developed conscience. Here you feel very little anxiety when you cause pain to others. Immoral behavior doesn't phase you at all. While you may conform to the standards of behavior of those around you, you do so just to "keep the peace" or keep out of trouble. You are not guided by a sense of what you believe to be right or wrong.

People with a weak conscience make the same mistake over and over again and do not benefit from the experience. They seldom really feel sorry for what they do and resent any effort made to punish them. In its extreme form this lack of conscience is called a "conduct disorder," as it frequently causes the person to be in trouble with authority figures or the law.

A Normal Conscience

Obviously, somewhere between the two extremes of an over and underdeveloped conscience there is a "normal" conscience. A normal conscience exists when there is a balance between the welfare of others and of oneself, so that a tension is created whenever either balance is disturbed. Such tension is not dominated by an exaggerated feeling of worthlessness about oneself, nor are the basic beliefs that underlie the conscience totally unfounded or irrational. The person with a "normal" conscience understands *why* something is right or wrong and does not condemn her or himself without an adequate basis in reality. For instance, one who *accidentally* fails to stop at a traffic signal, and then continues to feel depressed throughout the day because of the subsequent guilt, is failing to make some allowance for human imperfection. The person who *deliberately* drives through a traffic signal because he is in a hurry deserves to feel guilty afterward. Furthermore, if the resulting guilty feeling is unduly prolonged, even if the guilt is appropriate, this is also unhealthy. Here is the *essence of a healthy conscience*: it has the capacity to receive forgiveness and to benefit from the experience. To be able to give forgiveness to oneself is essential to *all* health.

In summary, therefore, I would say that a normal, healthy, and well-balanced conscience has the following qualities:

1. It is concerned with "morality" (the correct source of moral attitudes) and not with "moralism" (the preoccupation with right behaviors). Moralism is preoccupied with the "appearance" of correct behavior more than with the reason for it. What our parents teach us is usually mere moralism. Their underlying message is: "Do it this way and you will please me." Later in life we may still do things just to please our internalized parent without knowing *why* we do it. When the behavior is wrong, therefore, we feel guilty—even if a truly moral principle has not been violated. True morality, on the other hand, knows *why* something is wrong. Because it endangers the lives of others, it is always wrong to drive through a red traffic light without stopping. Throwing off the moralisms of our upbringing and developing a well-balanced morality is a necessary step

toward maturity and the freedom to experience our emotions in a healthy way.

As Christians, it is very easy to become engrossed in moralisms without understanding true morality. We can become preoccupied with behaving the "right" way, with no understanding of the underlying moral issues. By contrast, the gospel is *more* concerned with morality than with moralism. Righteousness has to do with the *source* of right behavior, with the motive behind the action. If the source is moral, the behavior will be righteous. If the source is not moral, no matter how perfect the behavior by outward standards, it will not be righteous by God's standards.

2. A healthy conscience should be flexible and not rigid, sensitive yet sensible. It should alert us to wrong just as pain alerts us to disease, but it should not proceed to punish us unmercifully for what we have done. It should respond to healing *quickly*. A well-balanced conscience should allow us to weigh all the factors involved in our wrongdoing, so that we can have an honest understanding of the limits of our responsibility. Could I have avoided what happened? Were there factors beyond my control? Was it really my fault? Can I easily rectify the wrong? A healthy conscience permits me to ask these sorts of questions and *listens* to the answers! An overbearing conscience condemns us *without* mercy or logic and allows no mitigating factors.

I am not suggesting that we should excuse wrong behavior. When we are guilty, we are guilty! I am calling for more truthfulness in our guilt. Excuses are often dishonest and are designed to "buy off" our conscience with deception. If we are really guilty, we should feel guilty and take the necessary steps to correct or repair our behavior.

3. A well-balanced conscience does not engage in excessive self-blaming, self-condemnation, or self-punishment. If we allow our conscience to do this, we destroy the learning value of the experience. Guilt is designed to correct behavior, not punish it; to bring us to repentance, not send us to hell. If we hurt someone with sharp words, we should learn not to do it again. If we fall prey to some immoral behavior, we should also learn from that experience. Guilt should serve as a warning sign that something is wrong—not as self-punishment. Preoccupation with self-blame and self-punishment does not facilitate healing and growth.

4. A normal conscience knows how to obtain and accept forgiveness, whether this forgiveness is to be from God or others, or from ourselves. In fact, we cannot stop self-punishment until we know how to obtain forgiveness. We must learn to trade our self-punishment for God's forgiveness. If someone we have harmed will not forgive us, we

can then receive that forgiveness from God. We must not let our failures continue to cast a dark shadow of guilt across our freedom and happiness. To punish oneself is to make a mockery of the Cross—you reject Christ's suffering for you. Christ wants to carry full responsibility for all our failures. Why not let Him do His work completely?

Neurotic Guilt

It takes an overdeveloped conscience to create "neurotic" guilt, but not everyone with a supersensitive conscience is neurotic. There are differences between a demanding conscience and having a guilt that is neurotic in the *degree* and *quality* of the tension it produces. Your guilt can be labeled as "neurotic" when it has the following qualities:

- You have a strong sense of your own evil.
- You feel guilty nearly all the time without adequate justification.
- You keep labeling yourself as "bad."
- Your guilt reactions last a long time.
- Your guilt is triggered by imagined wrongs, and then you cannot stop the guilt.
- Your guilt so incapacitates you that you cannot relate to anyone and want to withdraw.
- Your guilt causes you to want to take extreme actions (such as suicide) to remedy your wrongs.
- You cannot stop remembering all your past misdeeds.

Let me illustrate some of these. Let us suppose you become angry and shout at your son just as he is leaving for school. As soon as he walks out of the house, you experience great discomfort. Your guilt is sounding its alarm. Throughout the day you feel bad. You can't wait until you can do something to alleviate your guilt. When your son returns home you find some way to please him. You spoil him with a special treat or you are overly sweet to him.

If this happened repeatedly, it would be neurotic for the following reasons: First, you are not dealing with the cause of your anger (perhaps some disciplining would rectify your son's behavior far better than your anger), and second, you are teaching your son how he can manipulate you with guilt. Your guilt can be resolved with a simple apology and a clear statement about the behavior you expect, and not with an elaborate ritual of compensation. Directness and honesty are the product of a healthy conscience.

As another example, let's say that you have accidentally tramped on an insect and killed it. Suddenly you are overcome with a terrible guilt. "How could I do such a thing? Insects have a right to live as much as people! Couldn't I have looked where I was walking?" This sort of guilt over a ridiculous standard of behavior (which is not uncommon) is clearly neurotic. While it doesn't always take the form of insect killing, there are many parallels—like bumping other people's automobiles or putting an aged and sickly dog to "sleep." We ask ourselves, "Could I not have avoided that?" We make no allowance for accidents, and even if we do respect insect life, we cannot walk through a garden without harming it in some way. Life is full of risks, minor and major. To live is to cause some harm to something. Neurotic guilt is, therefore, frequently characterized by no actual violation, or the violation is of petty, internalized, or irrational principles. These can have a powerful negative effect on us, removing our freedom and robbing us of happiness.

Neurotic guilt can especially be caused by imagined violations. I know someone who often fantasizes that he is punishing those who have harmed him. He imagines placing them against a wall and mowing them down with a machine gun. When he is finished mutilating them, an intense guilt sets in. Even though he has not actually done any harm, he ends up with intense guilt feelings. As you can imagine, naturally, his problem is much more serious than just a disturbed guilt mechanism!

While many readers may not experience guilt to this extreme, there are subtle traps of a neurotic quality that can still imprison them. Perhaps you engage in the following self-talk: "I *must* do this"; "I *should* do that"; or "I've just *got to* go there." It's just possible that you are being controlled and manipulated by what you think others will say, or you have an exaggerated fear that you will not please someone. Whenever you violate one of these expectations, you feel terrible and engage in self-condemnation. While some "shoulds," "musts," and "oughts" in life are necessary, they are usually arbitrary and irrational. You need to carefully evaluate them before you respond to them. Strangely, when they are legitimate, they never feel like "shoulds."

The irrational "shoulds" we lay on ourselves rob us of freedom. Fortunately, we hold the key to unlocking these prisons and can, with careful thought and attention to the principles I am enunciating here, free ourselves from neurotic guilt.

Some Important Determiners of Guilt

Developing and maintaining a healthy conscience and appropriate guilt responses are not things that happen automatically. The underlying beliefs and attitudes require constant cultivation and weeding. You can pass through your childhood unscathed and then find that you fall prey in early adulthood (or any later stage of your life, for that matter) to influences that increase your guilt-proneness.

In Christian circles there are three important determiners of an aggravated conscience. These are:

1. An inadequate God concept
2. An inadequate sin concept
3. An inadequate forgiveness concept

Anyone reared in an environment where these inadequate concepts are propagated will find her or himself prone to guilt problems in later life. The concepts shape our belief systems very profoundly.

I was introduced to some distortion of these concepts shortly after my conversion at age eighteen. Through the influence of a friend I developed a very distorted idea of God's anger, believing that God wanted to punish all sin, even if He also wanted to forgive. As a result I experienced a marked increase in my guilt proneness which lasted for nearly five years before I finally became aware of the distortion in my understanding of God's nature. Rather than my early Christian experience being happy and fulfilling, it became burdensome and depressing. I look back now and regret that there wasn't some insightful person to correct my erroneous idea. At least two of my close friends (who were converted at the same time) fell victim to a similar erroneous idea and became so depressed by the experience that they gave up on their commitments. As far as I know, they have not returned to the Christian faith since then.

Allow me to comment on each of these concepts.

1. *An Inadequate God Concept.* We hardly ever pause to reflect on how we think about God, or our "concept" of God. We assume that everyone believes the same as we do. For some years now I have researched the variability of how different Christian groups think about God, and this has confirmed my contention that all Christians do not have the same ideas. There are many differences in their understanding of the nature of God.

For example, if you examine the concept of God as seen by missionary groups, ministers, and lay people of various denominations, you will find that each group, even within the same denomination, has markedly different beliefs. Women have a different concept of God from men. There are also marked differences in age, type of ministry, and cultures. Each produces quite different ideas about the nature of God. The net result is that we all end up in adult life seeing God somewhat differently. This difference is not always important, but it can have profound influences on our emotional health.

Your God Is Too Small by J. B. Phillips is a most important book on this topic. Phillips warns us to be careful about how we construct our image of God. If our understanding of God is that He is nothing more than a policeman, or if God is seen as harsh and punitive, we may experience considerable guilt-proneness.

As I have worked with people who have an inadequate God-concept, it has become obvious that they have merely internalized images of their parents, usually the father. If he has been harsh and punitive, they tend to see God this way.

2. *An Inadequate Sin Concept.* Guilt problems can also arise when we do not have a clear understanding of the nature of sin. Our conscience can bother us even when no sin has been committed. We feel guilty about many things, and not all can be classified as sin. Frequently, guilt over social rules and mores is only relevant to one culture. They do not apply in another culture and therefore are not absolute. Yet we label the breaking of these rules as "sin."

We can easily make our consciences into a god. I am familiar with the customs of some of the tribes of southern Africa and know how new missionaries have had great difficulty in adapting to the different "sin" standards of these people. They cannot understand why a man who is an avowed Christian would "take" food belonging to someone else and not see it as "stealing." In these cultures, food is viewed as common property and not "owned" by anyone. Food is the property of the community and can be taken by anyone in need of it. The western missionary's concept of sin is confusing to them. Their assumptions are relevant to their home culture, not the mission field.

I doubt whether everything *we* label as "sin" is actually sin in God's eyes. On the other hand, there may be many other actions we do not recognize as "sin." Prominent psychologist Karl Menninger once wrote a book called *Whatever Became of Sin?* In it he asked why we have dropped this concept from our psychological vocabulary. We need to be "on guard" against minimizing the sin concept in our eagerness to resolve our guilt problems. We run as much danger of creating an inadequate sin concept by minimizing sin, as we do when we overly exaggerate it.

3. *An Inadequate Forgiveness Concept.* Forgiveness is the genius of Christianity. It is the heart of the gospel—and the essence of Christ's substitutionary death on the cross. No other religious

belief system places it as central as the gospel does. What else is the Cross about? God knew when He created us that we would need forgiveness from Him and from others. It is for *our* benefit. I have a sneaking suspicion that most Christians have the irrational idea that perhaps God needed to forgive more than we needed His forgiveness. It's true that He *wants* to forgive us more than we are willing to receive it. When we have sinned or our conscience is bothering us, we need forgiveness. God's forgiveness must be preceded by repentance. God has provided forgiveness because *we* need it. This is the only way we can deal with our consciences, whether they are healthy or not.

Leslie Weatherhead, the famous English preacher, once said, "The forgiveness of God is the most powerful therapeutic idea in the world. If a person can really believe that God has forgiven him, he can be saved from neuroticism." To this I say a loud "Amen!"

Summary

Despite the centrality of forgiveness in the Christian gospel, guilt problems are prevalent among Christian people. The foundation for these problems is laid in early childhood. It is possible to come into adulthood with an overdeveloped or an underdeveloped system of guilt. An abnormally sensitive conscience can give rise to guilt feelings that 1) do not respond to forgiveness (whether from people or God); 2) do not cause us to make constructive amends; and 3) are the product of moralism (concern for surface behavior) and not morality. Neurotic guilt, that is, guilt that cannot receive forgiveness, tends to be vague and pervasive. It responds to the slightest provocation, often becoming preoccupied with self-condemnation and self-punishment.

To develop a healthy guilt response, you must challenge your irrational internalized do's and don'ts, thus developing a more rational and flexible conscience, a right attitude to failure, and the courage to take responsibility for mistakes without engaging in self-punishment.

For emotional freedom from neurotic guilt it is essential to have *a healthy God concept,* where God is not seen just as a policeman waiting to punish; *a healthy sin concept,* where one's conscience does not become a god and where one's understanding of sin is properly informed by the truth of Scripture; and *a healthy forgiveness concept,* where the true meaning of what God has provided is fully understood.

Additional Reading

1. *Your God Is Too Small,* J. B. Phillips (New York: Macmillan).
2. *Guilt-Free,* Dick and Paula McDonald (New York: Grosset & Dunlap).
3. *Overcoming Anxiety,* Archibald D. Hart (Dallas: Word Books).
4. *The Guilt Trip,* Hal Lindsey (Grand Rapids: Zondervan).
5. *Guilt and Grace,* Paul Tournier (New York: Harper & Row).
6. Romans 5.

9

Freedom to Love

A popular song of a previous generation has words that go like this: "Loving you is easy, 'cause you're beautiful. . . . " It is set to one of those melodies which haunts you all day long. Even now, as I am reminded of it, it has hooked me again, and it will be tomorrow before I will have set it aside. It is a beautiful song. But what an indictment against our society! Its message is: "It's easy to love you—*because* you're beautiful."

I am not disagreeing with the lyricist. In fact, I'm in full agreement. Lovely people *are* easy to love. Nice people are a joy to be around. These words are absolutely true, and that's the tragedy. The lyricist is just telling it as it is.

What's my gripe? Simply this: what if you're not beautiful? What if you don't turn eyes or attract attention to your physique or to your psyche? What if you are a bit abrasive or independent? What if you have little to offer in return, if you're just ordinary? Can you still expect to be loved? Do you have the prospect of lots of friends, as people fall over themselves to get to know you? I doubt it. If I were to judge by the desperate hunger of the many who have passed through my office, I would have to conclude that we are a love-starved society, and this starvation is due primarily to three factors: 1) we don't know what love is; 2) we don't know how to love; and 3) we love for the wrong reasons.

The result is that we can only love when it's easy and when there's a payoff. We can love when the object we love is "beautiful" or makes us feel good. This makes it both easy and profitable. We can love when we get something in return. "Be nice and loving to my mother. You know she's left us something in her will!" This is the characteristic of our age. We hardly notice how ulterior our motives are any more.

The Importance of Relationships

We cannot consider the topic of love without thinking of people and relationships. There are those, of course, who are so disillusioned about finding love in other human beings that they invest all their love in pets. Animals can provide a rich source of unconditional acceptance, so necessary for the satisfaction of our love needs. But we cannot isolate ourselves from people without paying for it in distorted personalities and disturbed priorities.

The most important thing we do as social creatures is *relate*. It is not work, nor is it fulfilling our ambitions. It may be difficult and cause much pain, but relate we must—and with other people.

Most of what I have discussed thus far is connected to how we relate to people. Our emotions never occur in a vacuum. They take place within the realm of our social interactions. Emotional problems are nearly always tied to some aspect of our relationships. This is what love is all about. At our core, we need to know how to give and how to receive love. Unless you can do this you are an incomplete person. You will never be fulfilled nor deeply satisfied until you are free to love.

Human relationships can also be the source of the most intense misery, and many people are unhappy and lonely because they cannot establish and sustain adequate social relationships. Most suicides, for instance, are over broken or unsatisfactory relationships, as are most divorces. However we look at it, relationship problems boil down to knowing how to love. When we can healthily love, human relationships become the source of deep satisfaction and lasting happiness. There is nothing to compare with it. Kings have surrendered their thrones for love.

Love Christian Style

There are many things you can do in isolation—but being a Christian is not one of them. If you hate people, better not become a Christian. Actually, that's not quite true. If you hate people, the *only* way to go is to become a Christian. You will discover a new way to love others.

I am convinced that the New Testament's emphasis on love is intentional. In contrast to the Old Testament, love permeates every page of the New. Every Gospel and every Epistle has something to say about love. Why? I think for two reasons:

1. *God knows us.* He knows we are primarily social creatures and He knows what we need. Our deepest needs will only be satisfied if we follow His prescription.

2. *The gospel has no meaning and no relevance outside the context of relationships.* It is here that we glorify God. It is here that His purpose is fulfilled. God demands that we love one another—it is

not optional. "He that loveth not knoweth not God . . . " (1 John 4:20 KJV). "If a man say, I love God, and hateth his brother he is a liar . . . " (1 John 4:20 KJV). Thus, both because God knows us and because His gospel depends on it, we are obligated to come to terms with love.

Don't make the mistake of thinking that because you are a Christian you know everything there is to know about love, however. True, you've been exposed to the ultimate demonstration of love, but implementing it in your life—to your neighbor, friend, husband, wife, and children—is another story. If you are having problems here, take heart. So do all of us. With a better understanding of what love is, you should be able to find freedom in giving and receiving love.

Misconceptions about Love

No psychologist or philosopher has thus far been able to define love adequately and to everyone's satisfaction. Though love is difficult to describe, all of us have experienced it enough to be able to recognize what it is.

The problem of defining love arises because of its complexity. There are *many* kinds of love and many ways of giving and receiving love. We are not concerned here with the romantic or sexual aspects of love, legitimate as these may be. They fulfill very real and deep needs in all of us and should not be lightly discarded. Even these forms of love, however, depend for their satisfaction on a much deeper long-lasting emotion called "true love."

The Greeks had different words for different types of love. I prefer not to separate them, as it is my strong conviction that *all* forms of love have a common thread around which they are woven to make a particular pattern we call love. The romantic and the sexual threads do not have to be present in true love. Frequently they only confuse the picture and make it more difficult to learn how to really love. But romantic and sexual love can never be complete without *true* love.

The only way to know what true love is, is to experience it. It has recognizable components: it is positive, accepting, and caring; it is affection combined with appreciation and respect. Words are incapable of adequately symbolizing or describing it.

Perhaps a better way of explaining love is to point out what it is not. Misconceptions about the nature of love abound and often create problems. Let's look at a few common misconceptions so as to clarify what true love really is.

- *"Love is feeling."* This is such a commonly held misconception that I want to dispel it right at the outset. What is implied here is that love is some sentimental knot in the stomach that takes away one's appetite and is only present if something special goes on inside whenever you are near the object of your love. Or, love is something you experience which is intensely strong and draws you to the other person with a force that is difficult to resist. These ideas, though often experienced, are not what love is about. Love may or may not generate a certain type of feeling. But mostly, feelings are the *consequence* of loving. We ought to feel a certain way toward someone *because* we love, not the other way around.

The damaging effects of seeing love mostly as a feeling are devastating in the area of marriage. All couples, I suppose, get married because they "feel" something in their love toward their partner. After a while this feeling may diminish or even go away. The conclusion one or both partners comes to then is that they are no longer "in love." Love is seen to be identical to the feeling.

This expectation for some feeling to be present in love has caused our society to develop a unique view of marriage in which there is a strong demand for a "relationship of togetherness." It requires that there be a high degree of sharing and intimate relating. The successfulness of this sharing and intimacy determines the stability and longevity of the marriage. No intimacy, no marriage, because the partners see love as synonymous with this intimacy.

The placing of so much value on "shared intimacy" (the demand for closeness and certain love feelings) places a strain on marriage not conceived of in earlier times and certainly not seen in all cultures. Unfortunately, shared intimacy is equated with that "special" romantic feeling. When the feeling goes away, the interpretation is that there is no love remaining and, therefore, the marriage should be dissolved.

This is a *low view* of love and marriage. It is no wonder that so many marriages can't hold together.

It is quite true that in the early stages of a romantically based relationship, love feelings predominate over everything else. We "feel" a special way toward the other person. But this is only a part of the total "love picture." True love has at least two other components to it: 1) respect and acceptance, and 2) certain behaviors toward the loved person. These are represented in Figure 6 on page 127.

Without these additional components, love feelings are meaningless. In fact, they can be so selfish that I doubt whether they represent love at all. *Lust* would be a better label.

Now I am not saying that romantic love, or special love feelings, are wrong. These feelings are wonderful while they last. What I am

Figure 6

The Dimensions of Love

saying is that true love is *more* than these feelings. Whether the love is for a child, a special friend, or a spouse, love *must* have more than mere feeling to sustain it. Let us briefly examine these two additional components.

1. Respect and acceptance.

It stands to reason, doesn't it, that a man who merely feels passionate toward a woman, but doesn't respect her or show her acceptance, is *not* in love with her, no matter how intense the passion. Respect and acceptance will often take time to develop. It needs intimacy and encounter as its soil in which to grow. This is why flings or one-night stands can never amount to anything. Love can only blossom when passion is under control. Often it is only when passion begins to subside that real love can begin to take root. Respect and acceptance, therefore, are closer to true love than passion.

2. Behavior toward the loved person.

If you examine 1 Corinthians 13 carefully, you will notice that everything described as "love" (which is the meaning of the word "charity") is *not* related to feelings, but to the two components I am discussing here. In particular, love is seen as *behavior.* Nowhere does 1 Corinthians 13 talk of love as a feeling. The priority is on what we *do* to others: kindness, long-suffering, peacemaking, and so on. Read it for yourself and check this out.

I strongly believe that loving behavior creates love feelings—more than the other way around. When a husband says to me, "I don't feel that I'm in love with my wife anymore," I usually ask: "When did you last behave toward her *as if you loved her?*" I then request that the husband begin to act lovingly and see what happens. Frequently I see something remarkable happen. The husband reports that he feels better toward her. As soon as partners start behaving toward each other as if they are still in love, they begin to report that the feeling of love comes back. When they start being kind, patient, tolerant, unprovoking, and "loving," they feel their love again.

This has led me to ask whether the feeling dimension of love is the *consequence* of loving behavior rather than its *cause*. In other words, which comes first, feeling or behavior? I vote for behavior!

Prove this quite easily for yourself. It works both ways. You can create or destroy love by your behavior. Find someone you don't love and start treating him or her as if you do. Very soon (it's almost alarming how quickly) you will begin to see your respect building and the feeling of love will emerge. The reverse is also true. Find someone you love and treat them as if you don't—and you will soon see your love vanish. On second thought, don't try the latter experiment. You may lose the one you love. But it does make my point.

• *Loving or liking?* The second major misconception about love confuses "loving" with "liking." Our lives are full of people we don't like: neighbors, work colleagues, and even relatives. We don't like their habits, their mannerisms, their looks, the way they walk, talk, and even smell. Mostly we don't like them because we suspect that they don't like us. But for the moment let us assume that there are those we genuinely don't like because of who they are.

You ask, *"Must* I love them even though I don't like them?" My answer is *yes!*

Again you ask, "Is it possible to love someone you don't like?" My answer is, *absolutely yes!*

"Can't I just ignore those people I don't like?" *No.*

"But I don't see how I can love someone I don't like."

Then hear me out!

We are called to *love* one another, not to like each other. I am so thankful for this! In fact, we are commanded to love the very objects we *don't* like. "Love your enemies," we are told. "Do good to them that despitefully use you." Can we *like* those who have hurt and discomforted us as their prime objective toward us? Obviously not. But we *are* called to *love* them.

I prefer to think of "liking" as a bonus. I may have to love someone I don't like. If I like what I love, I am very fortunate. It's the icing on the cake. This is all the more reason why we must not get hung up on the "feeling" component of love. Love is what we *do* to and for each other. The feeling will take care of itself. If I love you, my enemy, I will soon begin to feel compassion, kindness, and respect for you. I can't help it; it's as if there were a law built into me that commands it.

• *Loving and hating.* "If I hate someone, I couldn't possibly be able to love him." Believing that love and hate are opposites (so that if you have the one, you can't have the other) has probably led to more breakups of relationships, especially marriages, than we realize.

It is erroneous to believe that because you hate someone you can't also love him or her. The truth is that when you hate someone, you also have a great capacity to love that person. The reverse is also true. If you love someone, you also have a great capacity to hate that person.

Do you remember the song, "You Always Hurt the One You Love"? Well, this is very close to the truth. When you truly love somebody, you invest a lot of your being in that person and become extremely vulnerable because of the trust and commitment you make. If that trust if violated, you experience considerable emotional pain, and this can create intense hate feelings. That's why the more you love, the greater is your potential for hate. This is represented in Figure 7.

You will see that *love* and *hate* are together at one end of the pole because they are not really opposites but go together. At the other end are *fear* and *indifference*. These two go together just as love and hate do.

It is important to see that fear, not hate, is the true opposite of love. "There is no fear in love; but perfect love casteth out fear . . . " John

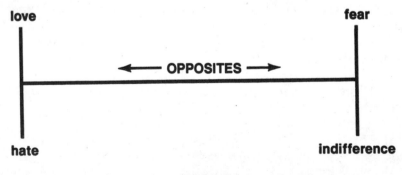

Figure 7

The Relationship Between Love and Hate

tells us in 1 John 4:18 (KJV), thus setting fear as the opposite of love. Paul writes to Timothy: "For God hath not given us the spirit of fear; but of power, and of love, and of a sound mind" (2 Timothy 1:7 KJV).

When you fear people, you can't love them. This is clear because love and fear can't co-exist. But notice that it is love that casts out our fear. Again, it seems to me, we see here the same message: if you *act* out of your love, the feeling (of fear, in this case) takes care of itself.

Just as fear is the opposite of love, indifference is the opposite of hate. At least when you hate someone, you care enough about him or her to have the intense feeling of hate. But when you're indifferent, the other person doesn't mean enough to you even to create any feeling of ill-will. Love cannot be present when there is indifference.

How do we generate love toward those we hate? Jesus tells us in the Sermon on the Mount, "Love your enemies . . . *do good* to them that hate you" (see Matthew 5:44 KJV). In other words, *behave* as if you love your enemy, and the feeling of hate will take care of itself.

What I have said thus far has important implications for marriage relationships. Too often, and too easily, couples conclude that their marriage is over merely because they perceive hate feelings between them. They interpret this as the end of their love. They fail to realize that when there is hate, there is probably a great capacity for love. To transform hate into love they should begin to behave as if they love each other again, and see this work miracles for their feelings. If your hate perpetually gets in the way, it means that you don't know how to love. You may need professional counseling from a pastor or psychologist to help you understand why you are so full of hate.

If you are caught in the fear-indifference trap, your situation is less hopeful and may need competent help to resolve it. Fear often has a basis in reality that needs to be identified and removed. Love *can* cast out fear and indifference. You *can* re-create the warm, accepting, and positive feelings that you so much desire. Again, you have to put action to your love and start behaving as if you love your partner.

The Early Roots of Love Problems

Why do some find themselves with major love problems in adult life? Why do so many find it difficult either to give love or to receive it? The answer lies clearly in the early experiences of the person, especially the childhood years.

To make up for love deficiencies acquired in childhood, many will resort to defensive strategies and their subsequent personalities, to a large extent, are shaped by and reflect these strategies. "Capturing" love may become a major life project for them. Everything they do and say becomes focused on this.

How we experience love in our childhood years plays a major role in shaping who we become. A person who is deprived of love for a prolonged period during the first or second years of life can become psychologically stunted. Babies can lose weight and become lethargic if love-deprived, as if some defense system has alerted them to the threat of abandonment. Nature knows how to protect the baby in a hostile environment and would rather cause it to die than leave it where it cannot be loved and nurtured.

As the child becomes more consciously aware of love in early childhood, the potential for psychological damage continues. The child wants and needs love. If given unconditional love, it will develop a mature understanding of how love is given and received, and a stable and secure feeling is thus created. This can occur even when the environment is unsatisfactory, as in ghetto areas or in times of war. Somehow, love shapes and protects the personality, and breeds security under all conditions, no matter how adverse.

If, however, the child is rejected and unloved or hurt, severe conflict ensues. This conflict can be created simply through inconsistency or the unpredictability of love. When double messages are sent like, "I love you—but I also hate you," or "I'll only love you if you obey me," they can be very evocative of deep-seated insecurity.

When conflicts are severe, the child is placed in a "doublebind" situation where he is invited to receive love but is punished instead. This produces the severest of all mental disorders and, according to some theorists, is a major trigger for schizophrenia. Certainly, many dissociative states can be shown to have their origins in early childhood love conflicts.

I certainly don't want any reader at this point to engage in excessive self-diagnosis. We all suffer from some deficiency in love during childhood and most of us turn out O.K. The disorders described here are very severe and are seldom seen in everyday life. Children are remarkably resilient, and the effects of less or extremes of love conflict are seldom very severe. These minor psychological scars are corrected as we get older and learn to trust others. If you believe that you may be suffering from one of the more severe emotional disorders because of love deprivation, I strongly recommend that you seek professional help.

Of the less serious but still disturbing ways in which we try to cope with love deprivation the following are the most common:

1. *A tendency to seek for love by* . . .

- Excessively trying to please others.
- Continually putting oneself down and elevating others unrealistically.
- Becoming a "clinging person"—where the message is "Please love me," or "Please value me."
- Developing love "substitutes" such as extramarital affairs or falling in love repeatedly and very easily.

2. *The development of severe character traits which are deeply stamped into one's personality* . . .

- Excessive jealousy, where there is both an intense desire to be loved and a fear that the love will be withheld or lost.
- A tendency toward self-pity and misery that keeps oneself miserable over some lost love.
- Sexual immorality, where there is a desperate search for love through sex.
- Pervasive insecurity, where there is a constant need for reassurance and high anxiety over a loved one's absence.

3. *The creation of pain or illness to handle love deprivation* . . .

"Now you'll have to love me 'cause I'm sick [or I'm in pain]." Love is captured primarily through sympathy. The "illness" can, of course, be purely psychological—though it may ultimately cause legitimate disease through the psychosomatic mechanism.

These are some of the pathetic ways in which people try to deal with their love deprivations. If a child is deeply and unconditionally loved and not placed in conflict situations over love, he or she can be spared these problems in later life. Love is a stabilizing keel. Hidden beneath the water, its weight and shape is such that, no matter how strong the winds of trouble may blow, it will always right the ship and keep it on its way.

When a child is deeply loved at home, he can cope with teasing at school or with rejection by peers. A child who has a secure home base can surmount failure, poverty, or any deficiency in physical attractiveness or intellect. The sense of emotional security that love provides is deep and sure.

If a child is not loved at home, no amount of success at sports, school prizes, and acceptance by peers will compensate. This child will grow up love-starved and pathetically searching for love. I know of only one encounter that can adequately reverse and heal this distortion. It takes place at the foot of the Cross.

The Gospel and Love

The relevance of the gospel to the problem of love has been the theme of preachers for centuries. One of the unique features of Christianity is that it makes loving possible in the very face of rejection and persecution. In fact, central to the whole Christian understanding of love is the idea that love is *only* meaningful in the face of opposition and dislike. Jesus said, "For if ye love men which love you, what thank have ye? For sinners also love those that love them" (Luke 6:23 KJV). The call here is clearly to a much higher form of love than what we are accustomed to, a love that transcends barriers of hate, dislike, fear, and indifference. This is a love that has no desire for personal reward—knowing full well that all the reward that love has to offer is in its giving and not its receiving.

When I am confronted by clients who are non-Christians, I am frankly pessimistic about how they will deal with their love problems. What models can they use? Where will they get their definitions of love? What resources do they have to draw on? Sometimes this very dilemma has caused them to ask me, "Well, where do you get your love from?" and I have had the privilege of sharing my experience with them. Being a Christian can make a big difference in what you believe love is all about.

How does the gospel relate to the problem of love? I believe that the essence of its relevance is that it makes loving possible because of three new relationships—to God, to others, and to ourselves.

1. *Loving is possible because of a new relation to God.* Paul tells us that we are " . . . no more a servant, but a son; and if a son, then an heir of God through Christ" (Galatians 4:7 KJV). In the very next chapter he then lists LOVE as the first of the fruits of the Spirit.

God has demonstrated to the world that love can be unconditional and given to those who are undeserving of it, and we are heirs of that giving. There is only one way you can know what this is like—and that is to experience it for yourself.

2. *Loving is possible because of a new relationship to others.* Most of us have a hard time defining who our "neighbor" is when we hear Jesus say that we must love our neighbor (see Matthew 5:43). The Jews also had trouble, and that's why Jesus told the parable of the Good Samaritan (see Luke 10:30–37).

The point of the parable is that *everyone* is our neighbor, without exception. Even those who have been our traditional enemies. Other people can never seem the same once we have encountered God in Christ. Not only will we see them with different eyes, but we will love them for different reasons. No longer do we have to depreciate them in order to feel that we are worth something, nor do we have to act as if we love them just so they will love us back. Our love becomes unconditional because of the new relationship we have with others through Christ.

Have you ever wondered why it is possible to love animals so much more easily than human beings? Literally millions of people shower love and affection on a wide range of pets from dogs to little mice. I have always felt that there was something tragic about this. Not that we should stop loving animals. I just adore them, and there can be a lot of therapeutic value in having pets. A number of psychiatric facilities provide pets for patients to aid their healing. Having something to love and love you back can heal broken minds and put lives together again better than all the king's horses and men.

But why is it so much easier to love pets? I think it's because animals know only *one* way to love, and that is the *unconditional* way. And we can love them because they will always receive that love whenever it is given. They don't play hard to get or other games and don't set up subtle resistances. Even when we have scolded them or withheld their food, they will respond to the slightest show of affection with immediate pleasure and no hint of any desire to get revenge or hurt us back. Why, even a completely strange dog can come to you and receive love as if it were entitled to it. Wouldn't it be wonderful if people could do this also?

3. *Loving is possible because of a new relationship to ourselves.* Encountering God changes our relationship to ourselves. No longer are we our own worst enemies. Our self-image ought to undergo a drastic change. For the first time we encounter a mirror that is thoroughly reliable and completely free of any distortion. We see ourselves for what we are—forgiven, valuable, and precious. If we have been love-deprived, we find the source of all love. If we have lived our lives in a constant state of self-hate, we can now surrender this hate. If we have pathetically sought the approval of others so as to feel that we are worth something, we can stop this search. If a parent has dominated our lives and caused us to feel that nothing we do is good enough, we can "replace" this parent with the Father who is all loving and full of grace.

No longer need we relate to ourselves as we did before. No longer need we be self-destructive. We have been saved from ourselves—*we are free to love.*

Summary

We find it hard to give and receive love. The main reason is that we don't know what love is—and therefore we don't know how to love. Love is not just a feeling. A large part of love has to do with the behaviors we practice toward one another. A careful study of 1 Corinthians 13, the classic description of love, will reveal that it deals primarily with the *behaviors* of love. Love is action. Love is what we do to and for one another. The feeling dimension of love follows when we do loving things. Liking and loving must not be confused. We can love those we don't like, and in the act of loving we can come to like them.

Love and hate are not opposites but both aspects of love. The opposite of love and hate is fear and indifference. Where there is hate, there is a great capacity for love. Where there is love, there is a great capacity for hate.

We cannot love in the truest sense of the word until we have a new relationship to the Source of all love, to others, and to ourselves.

In closing, let me leave three further thoughts with you:

1. *Love is contagious.* Love begets love. If you feel that someone fears or hates you, then *you* should start the loving.

2. *Love and forgiveness go hand in hand.* If your desire to hurt back is strong, *before* you can begin to love you must first forgive.

3. *Loving others changes you.* You cannot stay the same when you begin to love—it's impossible. *You* will change also. All you ever want to be can be realized if you start loving.

Additional Reading

1. *Start Loving,* Colleen Townsend Evans (New York: Doubleday).
2. *The Art of Loving,* Eric Fromm (New York: Harper & Row).
3. *In His Steps,* Charles Sheldon (Old Tappan, New Jersey: Fleming H. Revell).
4. *The Greatest Thing in the World,* Henry Drummond (Old Tappan, New Jersey: Fleming H. Revell).
5. *Caring Enough to Confront,* David Augsburger (Glendale, California: G/L Regal Books).
6. *How to Get Along with Almost Anyone,* H. Norman Wright (Dallas: Word Publishing).
7. *Love Is a Decision,* Gary Smalley (Dallas: Word Publishing).
8. 1 Corinthians 13.

10

Freedom to Be Joyful

When I anticipate the first visit by a new patient I expect the session to be full of emotional pain. This is natural, I suppose. Why else do people consult a psychotherapist? They are usually in some pain or trouble. Sometimes it is internal—their own feelings are out of control. Sometimes a loved one is giving them pain, like a son who is into drugs or a husband who is having an affair.

But yesterday morning I experienced a most pleasant surprise. A lady had called to make an appointment some weeks ago. She is a missionary in South America and was anticipating passing through Pasadena on a visit to her daughter. She needed to see me, she said, about a personal matter.

So I naturally expected to meet someone who was in considerable pain. Perhaps depressed. Perhaps in conflict or experiencing a quandary about her mission society. Or perhaps she was going through a crisis of faith. These are the common problems that missionaries present when they return home on furlough.

At the appointed time I went to the waiting room to receive my new client. She was an attractive middle-aged woman, and she greeted me with a big smile. Obviously, I said to myself, she's not depressed. Depression I can usually diagnose at first glance. I can see it in the eyes. They are sad and droopy. But this lady looked cheery—not sad.

She settled into the comfortable client's chair, leaned forward and said, "This is one of the happiest moments of my life."

I was taken by surprise. I had my pen and therapist's notebook ready. I was going to take down symptoms and list problem areas. And the lady was telling me she was extremely happy! I could see the joy in her eyes. They sparkled and danced. And I was taken aback.

You can imagine how confused I felt. People don't go to a psychotherapist because they are joyful—they go because they are sad or in pain. What on earth could this lady be wanting to see me about?

Then her story began to emerge. About four years earlier she had attended a seminar I was teaching for missionaries about to go to the field. It was a seminar on stress and how to manage it. During the break she had talked to me about a personal matter, and I had given her some advice on how to deal with it. I don't feel free to say what the problem was, but this lady followed my advice and it opened up a whole new life for her. She was now married to an exceptionally fine pastor/missionary, and both were serving the Lord in a very needy part of the world.

"I have never been so full of joy," she remarked. "And now being able to tell you my story and thank you personally for the help you have given me causes me even more joy." She then went on to say that she wanted to spend the session simply expressing her great joy.

It was one of the happiest therapy sessions I have ever encountered. No tears (except of joy). No fears. No emotional pain. We only talked about joy, and how full the Christian life is of it when it is lived according to God's will. She related how in reading the last chapter of my book *15 Principles for Achieving Happiness* recently, she was overcome with a desire to visit with me and share her thankfulness for my helping her to seek God's will. She was quite willing to pay the normal therapy fee for the privilege. I declined to accept payment. Moments of joy like this cannot be measured in fees. We parted, but she left behind a little bit of heaven's sunshine and quite a few questions about joy for me to ponder.

Why aren't Christians more joyful? Why do we live under clouds of disappointment or cynicism when the sunshine above the clouds is radiant with joy, ready to break through? Why do so many who claim to be believers seem to be lacking in downright old-fashioned and obvious joy? Joy ought to be central to every Christian's experience. Why? Because Jesus said, "These things have I spoken unto you, that my joy might remain in you, and that your joy might be full" (John 15:11 KJV). True, Jesus was speaking these words to His disciples just before the Feast of the Passover when He knew His hour had come and that He would be leaving them. But His words are timeless. The disciples were soon to experience His departure—and the sense of abandonment and disappointment. We are called to live in troubled times also, with grief and rejection a part of our human experience. And His words, spoken through Scripture, are "to make our joy full" also.

What robs us of this joy? How do we find it? How do we feel and share it? These are the questions I will attempt to answer in this chapter. If we master every negative emotion and demonstrate perfect control over all our emotional pain, we may still not experience real joy. Joy is a special gift of God. Some of us never discover it.

What Is Joy?

This must be our starting point. Too many of us miss real joy in our lives because we don't recognize it.

Very few psychotherapists I know deliberately set as one of their goals for therapy to enhance a client's level of joy. Secular psychology hardly ever addresses this emotion, presumably because so little is known and understood about joy outside of faith in Christ. They know about "peak experiences," such as conquering a mountain or accomplishing some great success, but this is not what joy is about. They know about ecstasy and intoxication, whether it is produced by power over others or artificial substances, but good, clean, pure, and unadulterated joy is foreign to them.

What then is joy? Webster's *New World Dictionary* says it is a very glad feeling, a happiness or a delight. At the root of the word "joy" is the idea of *rejoicing*. This is the central thought in joy. To have joy is to have something to rejoice about, to be extremely thankful for.

When the missionary lady sat down in my office and began to say, "I am not here because I have a problem, but because I am full of joy," she was in effect saying, "I am here because I have so much to rejoice over I cannot contain it." This is true joy. This is why so few temporal or earthly things give us joy. There is little to "rejoice" over, and even when there is something, it doesn't last very long.

One very important principle that Scripture illuminates for us is that "joy" is a fruit of God's Spirit (Galatians 5:22). It is the natural product that proceeds from the Spirit, just as fruit is the natural product of the root sunk deeply and firmly into soil. Read again this portion of Scripture from, say, verse 9 to verse 26 of Galatians 5. The apostle is contrasting the "works of the flesh" with the "fruits of the Spirit." The works of the flesh are sins against God's commandments, against our neighbors, and against ourselves. Our Christianity calls us not only to oppose the works of the flesh, but to bring forth the fruits of the Spirit, including joy. This is why in verse 25 he says, "If we live in the Spirit, let us also walk in the Spirit." This implies that some translation from a mere state of joy must take place into the "practice" of joy. Living must become walking. Ideas must become actions. Good intentions must become good deeds. The fruit is only ripened when it is ready to be plucked and moves on to serve some other purpose.

Why then do so many not manifest obvious joy? Perhaps it's because their "living" never becomes "walking." They never practice what they preach.

Joy, then, is a very special state of rejoicing—a condition of knowing and living out God's purposes through His Holy Spirit. It is not a feeling of ecstasy, though joy, when fully appreciated and experienced, may create a deep feeling of unexplainable happiness. It is not just being happy. Happiness is another step removed. Joy is more basic than happiness, though I believe that unless joy gives rise to a sincere and stable happiness it probably isn't real joy. Joy is less dependent on circumstances than happiness. Joy can exist even when everything, and I mean everything, is disintegrating around you, because joy is more an attitude of appreciation than it is a state of being.

Those secular psychologists who have dared to approach the topic of joy have done so by defining joy as the feeling that comes from the fulfillment of your potential. They claim that every living person has not achieved his or her full potential. Latent abilities, hidden talents, and underdeveloped capacities for excellence and pleasure lie dormant, by and large. This robs us of joy in living and prevents us from "reaching the unreachable star." To be joyful, therefore, one must fulfill more of one's potential, they tell us. The more potential you fulfill, the more joy you have. It builds a sense of confidence, enhanced self-esteem, and self-contentment, and a "winning" attitude.

There is *some* truth to these contentions. I think it is true that most, if not all, of us do not reach our full potential. We stunt our capacities, repress our feelings, and rob ourselves of the freedom to be fully alive. But it is precisely in this realm of "achieving our full potential" that the dangers of the "works of the flesh" lie. It is because we are seeking to "win over others" that we violate the command to be loving to them. In seeking the maximum potential for ourselves (and I believe this is quite legitimate within the bounds of what God plans for you) we easily become misled or misdirected, clamoring for more success or opportunity and clambering up and over the backs of others we have pushed down.

No, joy is not at the end of the rainbow of self-fulfillment. It is an ingredient given at the beginning—a gift that should foster grace and love as we seek to become all that God has planned for us to be. Joy is *not* a goal. It is a gift.

Obstacles to a Life of Joy

Not only should we clarify what love is, but a life of joy can only be achieved if you know how to avoid the "thieves" of joy. It is like running an obstacle race. Know where the obstacles are and how to avoid them, and you can win the race!

Interestingly, Scripture clearly identifies some of the obstacles to a life of joy. I will briefly discuss a few of these. I have observed them at work in my own life as well as in the lives of my clients.

• *Worldly cares*

Of all the thieves of joy, this one comes to my mind first. In the parable of the sower, Jesus tells how some of the seed fell among the thorns. He then says, ". . . and the care of this world, and the deceitfulness of riches, choke the word, and he becometh unfruitful" (Matthew 13:22 KJV).

I used to think that this parable only applied to evangelism. But it does not. The "care of this world" chokes the word no matter when it is heard or read. We can be so preoccupied with the here and now, so caught up in this life and its comforts and with fulfilling our personal ambitions that we literally choke the word out of us. And with it goes our joy.

We desperately need to balance our living in the present with our eye on eternity in these critical days. I would suggest that it is the maintenance of this balance that keeps us joyful. As soon as the scale tips too much toward our living in the world, our joy diminishes. Too much of an eye on eternity doesn't make me very useful here! We are better off, though, keeping the scale tipped slightly toward eternity.

• *Life's circumstances*

Psalm 126:5 has a wonderful promise: "They that sow in tears shall reap in joy." Many of life's circumstances are cause for tears. I cannot begin to tell you of the human pain and emotional suffering that so many must bear day by day. Their "captivity" (which is the context for this Psalm) is a life of hardship and endurance.

We may go through periods of our life when the waters are smooth and the wind is blowing at the right speed and in the right direction. But sooner or later life becomes tumultuous. Sickness and death cannot be avoided indefinitely, and bull markets don't last forever. All of life has the seeds of suffering and hardship. This is the given. How you cope with this hardship is what determines whether joy will be constant or fluctuate with your trouble.

The goal for mature living is to maintain a constant state of joy, no matter what the circumstances of life. And this *is* possible. In 2 Corinthians 6:10, Paul recounts how that it is possible to be ". . . sorrowful, yet always rejoicing; as poor, yet making many rich; as having nothing, and yet possessing all things."

This is the great paradox of joy. It can exist in all circumstances. One can be in grief over the death of a loved one, yet still be "in joy." One can be the target of malicious scandal, yet still be "joyful." All around may abandon you, yet you can rejoice in what is left—

and go on from there. This is the Christian's transcendent spirit. You ride on top of the storm, not under it. I have always been moved by the words of Acts 5:41: "And they departed from the presence of the council, rejoicing that they were counted worthy to suffer shame for his name" (KJV). What a spirit this is! What courage, what maturity!

How is it possible to be joyful in all circumstances? Go back to Psalm 126 again: "They that sow in tears shall reap in joy" (verse 5 KJV). The very next verse says: "He that goeth forth and weepeth, bearing precious seed, shall doubtless come again with rejoicing, bringing his sheaves with him" (v. 6 KJV). Notice, the seed becomes sheaves. It is sown, multiplies, and returns as an abundance.

Tears are seed. Sorrow and pain are seeds. Unhappiness is a weed, and it is not the same as sadness. Unhappiness is the product of immaturity. Sorrow or sadness is the inevitable fact of life. But each tear becomes a sheaf of joy. It is precious seed being turned into abundant joy by the Master Gardener. For a while the sorrow may prevail, but deep down there will be joy and the day will come when it breaks forth in glorious life again.

How do you keep that joy alive even when sorrow dominates? As I suggested earlier, through *rejoicing*. "The Lord hath done great things for us; whereof we are glad" (Psalm 126:3 KJV). Because he "hath" done great things, I can rejoice in the knowledge that even this present sorrow will bring forth abundant sheaves of joy again.

- *Worry and anxiety*

Here we have a destructive pair of emotions. They are especially destructive of joy!

Not all anxiety is bad for us. Some of it is good because it moves us to make amends or avoid destructive actions. But the form of anxiety we call "worry" is always bad.

Worry and joy *cannot* coexist. Worry extinguishes joy. Sometimes being joyful can help to eliminate worry, but this is not as easy as it seems.

I need to caution against a certain style of thinking and behaving which is quite prevalent in certain Christian groups. It is a form of denial that uses "praising" as a way of blocking out the reality of certain circumstances or for masking or covering legitimate concerns.

No doubt you've heard people say (or you've said it yourself), "I'm just not going to think about it." This is part of this style, but it goes further. The denial of very spiritual people includes such activities as praising God out loud, or of singing a hymn as a way of covering the worry or anxiety.

The only time such a practice is healthy is when you have adequately dealt with the source of the worry. You cannot sweep all worry under the rug. Some of it needs to be heeded and dealt with.

For instance, let's suppose you've noticed a lump in your armpit. You do nothing about it, and it gets a little bigger. You say to yourself: *It's no big deal. I'm not going to worry about it.* Every time you think about the lump, you break out in praise or song as a way of overcoming the worry. This is not healthy—either from a physical or psychological point of view. It's not healthy spiritually either! *First* get the lump attended to, and if there is nothing to be concerned about and you still find yourself worrying, then praise and sing your worries away.

The opposite of worry is *peace of mind.* A tranquil spirit is God's very special blessing, and it is intended for *all* of us. Jesus left us a special legacy here—very much like a last will and testament: "Peace I leave with you, my peace I give unto you; not as the world giveth, give I unto you. Let not your heart be troubled, neither let it be afraid" (John 14:27 KJV).

No matter what you sum together in this life, including all you can possess, achieve, or conquer, these do not add up to peace of mind. In fact, they may even be an obstacle to such peace. If so, then some may need to be set aside or renounced in order to more fully possess the peace we crave.

As I pointed out earlier, worry blocks out joy. On the other hand, peace of mind fosters joy. It is the perfect seed-bed for growing pure, abundant joyfulness. There is not much more I can say about creating this peace of mind. All I have written in this book is focused on creating this peace.

- *Hurried lifestyle*

There is not much said in Scripture about the role of overstress in destroying peace of mind and joy, yet I know it does so. I suppose I could quote Proverbs 19:2, ". . . he that hasteth with his feet sinneth," but that would be stretching it a little. It refers more to rashness and impulsiveness than the hurriedness of modern life.

Nevertheless, it is true. Hurriedness is potentially self-destructive and sinful.

The reason Scripture says little about this is simple: stress is a problem of twentieth-century living. In New Testament times there were other problems. Disease, abuse, and cruelty were common. But the pace of life was considerably slower. There were no supersonic jets or high-speed freeways to hasten our heartbeats and energize our adrenalin. You went to bed when it was dark and got up when it was light. Lack of sleep was hardly a problem!

But today we are all in a hurry. Pressure is greater now on the average citizen than at any other time in history so that a greater percentage of the population is suffering from the consequences of this pressure—stress/disease.

Now my focus here is not on stress, but the impact that being overstressed has on our joyfulness (or should I say joylessness?).

Overstress destroys joy in a number of ways:

- It robs us of time to be joyful.
- It depletes our natural brain tranquilizers and creates anxiety states.
- It distorts our perspective on life's circumstances so we cannot see what there is to rejoice over.
- It robs us of time to be with God. God needs us to slow down so that He can keep up His communion with us.

Unfortunately, hurriedness often makes us feel good. Adrenalin flows strong, and we feel vital and energetic. But this is a false feeling. In its shadow lurks disease, destruction, and depression. Real joy is not the same as an adrenalin kick—though few really see or feel the difference these days.

If you want to be full of joy, you will need to slow down. You will have to sleep more, play more, and spend time with your loved ones. You may have to settle for fewer stimulating and exciting activities and rediscover the elementary pleasure of boredom and the delight of simple things. You cannot buy joy nor will you find it in expensive cruises or luxury living.

I am always moved by a song from Camelot in which King Arthur and Guenivere ask the question: "What do the simple folk do?" You will recall that they are bored and "blue" and don't know what to say to each other. They are surrounded by wealth and every luxury imaginable, but they don't know how to be happy. So they sing a song, asking the question: What do the simple folk do to be joyful? The song doesn't come up with any profound conclusions, only singing, whistling, and dancing. But the message is still true. Simple things—for simple folks. There is profound wisdom in this. We could all benefit from returning to more elementary happiness-producing activities. Our joy will then be full again.

Joy and "Being"

In closing let me return to a point I made at the beginning: joy ought to be central to every Christian's experience.

Joy and "being" go together. They are inseparable. By "being" I mean being grounded in Christ, being rooted in the source of all joy. There is no real deep joy outside of this grounding.

The analogy of a plant growing in a garden comes to mind. The plant may be of a beautiful variety. It may be planted in the right place with the proper amount of shade and sunshine. It may be well watered and carefully pruned. But the roots better be in good soil or else it will not grow and blossom as it should. The joy of the Christian comes from the roots—and to be rooted or grounded in the life-giving soil of Christ is absolutely essential. Oh, you can eke out an existence in unfertilized soil or in dirt that is hard or stony. I have had such plants in my garden. They eventually all die. But when I transplanted them so that they can build roots in the life-giving rich soil of another part of the garden, their joy and beauty almost exploded before my eyes.

God has created us for Himself. He made us in His image, with the capacity to transplant ourselves to the transforming and life-giving soil of His Son. Who would not want to tap into this joy-full resource?

Summary

We have examined one of the most powerful of the positive emotions, the feeling of joy. It is a misunderstood emotion, many believing that it can be found in worldly pursuits or pleasures.

Joy ought to be central to every Christian's experience because Jesus said, "These things have I spoken unto you, that my joy might remain in you and that your joy might be full" (John 15:11 KJV). More often than not it is not central to our experience. We allow many distractions to rob us of joy. We surrender to our circumstances.

Additional Reading

1. *15 Principles for Achieving Happiness,* Archibald D. Hart (Dallas: Word Publishing).
2. *Be Joyful,* Warren W. Wiersbe (Wheaton: Victor books).
3. *Joy,* William C. Schultz (New York: Ballantine Books).
4. *Feeling Good about Your Feelings,* Barry Applewhite (Wheaton: Victor Books).
5. *Surprised by Joy,* C. S. Lewis (William Collins Sons & Co.).
6. *My Heart Sings,* Joan Brown (Dallas: Word Publishing).
7. Philippians 4.

11

Freedom to Be Real

"What is *real?*" asked the Rabbit one day, when they were lying side by side near the nursery fender, before Nana came to tidy the room. "Does it mean having things that buzz inside you and a stick-out handle?"

"Real isn't how you are made," said the Skin Horse. "It's a thing that happens to you. When a child loves you for a long, long time, not just to play with, but *REALLY* loves you, then you become Real."

You may recognize this quotation from Margery Williams' *The Velveteen Rabbit,* the fascinating and moving story of a velveteen toy rabbit who so much wanted to be real but didn't know what "real" was. The story moves us because it causes us to identify with the dilemma of the toy rabbit. It triggers a similar question to the one he asks: "What is *real?*" It forces us to ask, "Am I real?"

It is not only toys that want to be real; people want to be real as well! Does this seem strange to you? Compared to toys, we *are* real—or are we? It depends on what we mean by "real." The sense in which I want to use the word here relates to the deep longing we all have to become full, complete persons—people who know who they are and where they are going. "Real" means genuine. It is the opposite of pretend. It means genuine and authentic. We all want to be "real" in these meanings of the word.

There is a quality of one's being that seems to be *unreal,* almost make-believe. We often ask ourselves, "Is this really me? Is this all there is to me? Where do I fit into life? Am I in any way special?" We have a strong sense that we exist in order to become something or to fulfill some greater purpose, but we don't really know what this something or purpose is. Yes, the toy rabbit's dilemma strikes a resonant chord in all of us. It is an analogy to the deepest longings of all human beings.

Who Are You, Really?

One very prominent psychologist, Dr. Carl R. Rogers, has spent a lifetime trying to understand this question's dilemma. While I don't agree with everything that Carl Rogers has written in his approach to understanding human nature, he has a very important point of emphasis that we should not overlook. After thirty-three years in the psychotherapist's chair, encountering thousands of clients with their problems, he wrote this in *On Becoming a Person:*

As I follow the experience of many clients, in the therapeutic relationship which we create, it seems to me that each one is raising the same questions. Below the level of the problem situation about which the individual is complaining, behind the trouble with studies, with wife, or employer, or bizarre behavior, or frightening feelings, lies *one* central search. It seems to me that at the bottom each person is asking: Who am I, really?

While I don't believe that Dr. Rogers has all the right answers, I do believe that he is right when he gives pride of place to the question *Who am I, really?* And the whole process of "becoming real," of finding one's real self and claiming the right to be this self under God, is what most of life is all about. In some respects, this is what I have been trying to help you accomplish throughout this book. The process of becoming real is, I believe, what our Christian faith and walk are all about. It is a process (a sanctification, if you prefer) of finding yourself and, in a special sense, becoming authentic and genuine. I can think of no better words to describe it.

Our Unreal Selves

"I suppose *you* are Real," said the Rabbit. And then he wished he had not said it, for he thought the Skin Horse might be sensitive. But the Skin Horse only smiled.

Most of the time we deal with the outside world from behind phony facades. We wear masks. No one must know we aren't real, nor who we really are.

Why? Because we fear we won't be liked or accepted. Our culture prevents us from being real to the world. And the closer we are forced to live together, the more unreal we become and the more we hide from each other.

The way our society is now structured, with the majority of us living in urban areas where there has been an increased concentration of people in apartments and condominiums, is not conducive to greater freedom. Thrown together, with a population density unknown in previous times, we are rapidly losing our ability to get along with each other. Closeness has not improved our intimacy skills. If anything, we have become more skillful in finding psychological ways to "distance" ourselves from others and establish our privacy. It doesn't take bricks and mortar to build the most effective barriers of all between people—only psychological attitudes.

This diminished capacity for intimacy, despite our being forced to live closer together, has produced a quality of unreality in our relationships which is also unique to our age. It seems to me that when I was a child we knew more about the other people in our block than my children do today. There seems to be "distance." People want to be private. This is not conducive to becoming real.

Why are we so scared of being real to each other in close relationship? I have already suggested that it is because we are afraid that others won't like what they see in the real us. But it goes further than this. Is it possible that we cannot be real to others because we can't be real to ourselves? Because we are afraid of our deep inner selves, we won't reveal it to others. We fear what is hidden in the deep recesses of our personality. Why do we find it so uncomfortable when someone begins to be very honest with us about who we are? Because we are afraid of our real selves. We squirm, we conceal, we sweat, and we want to run away from such honesty. We resist being exposed to the real truth about ourselves, especially if it is not attractive or desirable. But if we can't be real to ourselves, we certainly can't allow ourselves to be real to others!

Back to the Velveteen Rabbit:

> For a long time he lived in the toy cupboard or on the nursery floor, and no one thought very much about him. He was naturally quite shy, and being only made of velveteen, some of the more expensive toys quite snubbed him. . . . Between them all the poor little Rabbit was made to feel himself very insignificant and commonplace . . . .

I think we all know this feeling.

We hide from our feelings. The struggle to become real is most evident in the area of the emotions, because it is here that we want to hide more than anywhere else. From our earliest years we are trained not to show our emotions—in fact, to be unreal. This is especially true for us males.

Recently I saw a client who described how she had been taught not to display her anger. For years she has gotten into trouble with members of her family, her friends, and her work associates, because she could not express her anger directly. She could only express it in passive, indirect ways like pouting or criticism. From her earliest years she was told that she should not show anger. "People won't like you if you become angry," her mother repeated over and over again. So now she expresses her anger by resistance, negativity, and sulking. Such behavior or inability to deal with anger makes us more "unreal."

Because we are taught *not* to show feelings, some of us declare war on them and begin a campaign of suppression and denial that turns us more and more into "toy" people with no authenticity and no heart. We dare not allow ourselves to feel, so instead of being spontaneous we become stunted and overcontrolled. Because we must always hide our true feelings, we become an enigma to others. Instead of developing transparency so that all may know who and what we are, we become a mystery. Instead of finding wholeness and emotional health, we become erratic and unpredictable. No one can trust us. After all, when one person plays at being a toy, others can't be real either.

We depend on one another for reality. Whatever else it takes to set our *real* selves free, it can only happen in the context of our relating to one another. There is no way we can become real in isolation. We need people to make it happen. We need real people to show us how to be real.

It seems to me that this is how God has ordained it, whether we like it or not. He expects us to be able to live together. Why else would He have had so much to say about love? And forgiveness? And caring? It is only in our living and loving with one another that real beings can grow.

An important lesson we are learning from the healing disciplines is that people who live in a real community become real in themselves. Place severely disturbed psychotics in an accepting and understanding community, and they start to get better. Surround an alcoholic with supportive and caring loved ones, and he can give up his alcohol. Communities, we are discovering, can be powerful and therapeutic change agents.

Our society at large does not provide much in the way of community. Look at the titles of the books our age is producing: *The Lonely Crowd, The Pursuit of Loneliness, Pathways to Madness.* All of them deal with the loneliness of our time. Much of this loneliness is due to the psychological barriers we put up against intimacy.

Why should this loneliness and psychological isolation prevent us from becoming real? Primarily because it prevents us from interacting and living in a safe and stress-free manner. We all need to be loved, feel secure, be recognized, and have companionship—and these needs can only be met satisfactorily when we have significant "others" with whom we can relate.

Our society is full of people who feel they are outcasts. Nobody really cares for them. If somebody does, it is usually because of a feeling of obligation, either through marriage or some family relationship. They do not feel love without some string attached to it. They never feel accepted unconditionally, but only with some obligation. Listen carefully to your neighbor or to that person who sits next to you at work. Their deepest heart cry is probably: "No one loves me without expecting something in return." Their message will be one of loneliness and alienation and a desperate hunger for understanding at a deep level.

Carl Rogers identified three conditions that had to be present for people to become "real" or fully authentic. These conditions should be present in childhood. If they are not, that child grows up with some distortion of his or her real self. These conditions are:

- Unconditional acceptance and warmth
- Empathic understanding
- Congruence or genuineness

These qualities *heal* people, so much so that Rogers calls them the "therapeutic triad." They provide a nonthreatening atmosphere in which people can explore and develop their true selves. Whenever relationships are characterized by these conditions and whenever communities foster these traits among their members, people are transformed from being artificial and phony into real people.

What actually happens when we begin to accept one another unconditionally with deep understanding and genuineness?

1. *We begin to experience, understand, and accept our feelings and desires that previously we would not consciously confront.* In our Christian communities, particularly, we tend to conceal our feelings of hostility and sexuality. Most of us live our lives feeling that we are hypocrites, fearing that others are not quite like us, and that our secrets will somehow be discovered. It can be a revolutionary experience to discover, in the context of understanding and acceptance, that we are *all* in the same boat. Others feel exactly like we do. Our fears are their fears.

2. *We begin to understand the reasons behind our behavior and feelings.* The really free person is one who knows and understands *why* he or she does and feels things. Such people have been able to get behind their masks, facades, and false fronts that have been erected even to themselves. Thus they come to know themselves better. The better we know ourselves, the better we can follow God's plan for our lives.

3. *We learn to be ourselves.* We discover that our real selves, despite their flaws and shortcomings, are all we have to offer to God and the world. So why not make the best of them? We stop fearing our deep selves and confront our weaknesses and failures honestly and with enough courage not to punish ourselves. This opens us to new and more positive forms of behavior, because our energy is being directed at reconstruction and modification, not self-destruction.

Who are you, really? You will only find out when you begin to encounter others with courage and openness. Start accepting others unconditionally, be understanding and genuine, and see if this doesn't pay off for you. You will be surprised how quickly others begin to do the same for you and you will soon be on the way to becoming real:

> The Rabbit sighed. He thought it would be a long time before this magic called Real happened to him. He longed to become Real, to know what it felt like; and yet the idea of growing shabby and losing his eyes and whiskers was rather sad. He wished that he could become it without these uncomfortable things happening to him.

Are Our Christian Communities Any Better?

Theoretically, our Christian communities should be the ideal places for making people real. If you examine Dr. Rogers's therapeutic triad closely, you will see that the conditions he is advocating as necessary for healing are all embraced by the New Testament concept of love. He probably got his ideas from what Scripture teaches about love. Love is all of the things that we know can heal: unconditional acceptance, empathy and understanding, and genuineness.

But Christian love is more than just these three qualities. What the gospel gives us is a *reason* to be loving with one another. Perhaps this is what is wrong with our society—people don't have a reason to be any other way than they are with one another. John reminds us that "we love him, because he first loved us" (1 John 4:19 KJV), and *because of this* we should love others. We cannot escape the principle: "Bear ye one another's burdens, and so fulfill the law of Christ" (Galatians 6:2 KJV). It is God's love for us, in Christ, that gives us the incentive to care for one another. Why else would we do it? Humanly speaking, the rewards for loving are not all that great!

But are our communities, our churches, our fellowships, our homes, our seminaries and colleges, loving and caring communities? You can only answer this for yourself. It would be unfair for me to generalize. I do know, however, that these communities are just as full of lonely, alienated, and outcast-feeling people as any secular community I have encountered.

Why is this? We are just as guilty of giving in to our natural inclinations to hurt back and isolate others as nonbelievers. We carry emotional scars from our past that get in the way of loving in the present. We have learned how to shield and protect ourselves from the penetrating, critical eyes of insecure people.

Over the years I have counseled with many hurting people, both Christian and non-Christian. Sadly, many Christians are no more "real" than others. We have no cause to be content with what is happening in our churches. There is as much callousness, inconsideration, and selfishness here as anywhere. It is often more easily concealed behind pseudo-spiritual talk and phoniness. And this is not the fault of the gospel. If the blame is to be placed anywhere, it must be placed squarely on ourselves. After all, the clay can resist the loving hands of the Great Potter.

We have made our mistakes—so let's learn from them. The incentive to love and care for one another is always renewable, so let's remove whatever hinders us. We have the power of God to transform our callousness, inconsiderateness, and selfishness. With God's help it can become real acceptance, understanding, and genuineness—so let's tap into the Source and utilize it to make up for the deficiencies and inadequacies of our past. If you don't have a reason to love, perhaps the problem is that you have never experienced His loving first. This, then, is where you should begin.

Weeks passed, and the little Rabbit grew very old and shabby, but the boy loved him just as much. He loved him so hard that he loved all his whiskers off, and the pink lining to his ears turned grey, and his brown spots faded. He even began to lost his shape, and he scarcely looked like a rabbit any more, except to the Boy. To him he was always beautiful, and that was all that the little Rabbit cared about.

What Are the Characteristics of a Real Person?

The Rabbit could not claim to be a model of anything, for he didn't know that real rabbits existed; he thought they were all stuffed with sawdust like himself, and he understood that sawdust was quite out-of-date and should never be mentioned in modern circles.

As I have already mentioned, it is primarily in the area of the emotions that the struggle to become real predominates. What are the characteristics that influence this struggle and how can you move toward reality? I will only discuss three: authenticity, integrity, and adaptability.

Authenticity. This implies that there is consistency between what you are and what you pretend (or even believe) yourself to be. It is the result of knowing yourself realistically, not hiding any aspect of your being from yourself, and then being true to what you really are. Authenticity can only exist when you stop imitating others and when you are not overconcerned about the impression you make on them.

Phoniness is the opposite of authenticity and is characterized by a strong need to imitate the feelings, ideas, values, or attitudes of others. Sometimes these "others" are our parents, but often they are the significant group with whom we relate.

To some extent, we all feel a little phony. It's a part of our feeling of unreality. We feel inadequate and helpless when we try to be true to ourselves. We are afraid that people won't like what we really are. In becoming a real person we invariably discover that when we drop our masks and reveal our true selves to the world, we are more accepted, *no matter what we reveal.* It is our masks that people don't like, not our true selves.

Consider for a moment the qualities of someone you really admire. Write them down. It is my guess that, nine times out of ten, what you admire most is their authenticity, their genuineness. What they are, and what they *say* they are, are highly congruent. "What you see is what you get!" Why, then, is it so difficult for *you* to be yourself? If you admire this trait in others, you should begin to risk being your authentic self.

I talked recently with a minister who described how he was struggling to measure up to the standards of his senior pastor whom he considered to be a model. The younger man agonized over his sermon preparation, trying to be as good as his senior, and followed the rules for good sermon making as he had learned them in seminary. But he was not succeeding.

Somehow, something was missing. He prayed earnestly, but he felt he could never match up, no matter how hard he worked at it. So I asked him, "Have you ever tried just being yourself?" He was quite taken aback. What did I mean? I told him that he was a man with much to offer. His life had been full of experiences of both success and failure.

My advice to him was simply this: "Stop trying to imitate or compete with someone else, and let your true self come through in what you have to say." Sermon techniques must be subservient to authenticity, and if he could achieve this I felt strongly that he would feel better about his preaching. It did not take long. His unique and individual style was quite beautiful—and he became a very effective preacher in his own special way.

Each of us needs to be ourselves. Being different we must discover the freedom of our individuality. God did not cast us all in the identical mold, so why should we want to become like someone else?

The key to authenticity is to *be true to yourself.* Discover who and what you are through honest dialogue with trusting and accepting friends, and then present this to God for His review and blessing.

Integrity. Integrity is doing the right thing when no one else is there to judge. It is being complete and undivided. If you cannot keep the law when no policeman is around, you probably do not have integrity!

To have integrity means that you are responsible, reliable, and dependable. You believe the values you live by. Integrity means more than honesty. It implies a quality of soundness and safety (that others can trust). When you are among people of integrity you feel absolutely safe.

Adaptability. Life is like the wind. It can change direction without warning and is forever demanding that we adapt to its change. To cope effectively with life we must be adaptable and resilient.

Adaptability implies that you can modify your style of life, your expectations, and coping behavior to accomplish your goals. Psychotics are not adaptable. They stick rigidly to their delusions and resist any hint that they should change. Neurotics are less adaptable than normal people. They persevere with faulty behaviors or erroneous ideas and their behaviors are erratic. They make the same mistake over and over again without learning from the experience.

To be adaptable one must live in the present and be willing to face the stark reality of life. You must also believe that you can, with God's help, control your life.

Resilience is what makes rubber different from any other physical material. When you stretch it, it returns to its original shape. Have you ever played with one of those "green monster" toys that you can stretch and twist beyond all recognition? When you let it go, it returns to its original shape with no sign of damage. That's resilience. Without it, life is tragic. To be resilient means you can "bounce back" when life distorts you. When you receive a hard blow and your world seems to crumble, you recover your composure, pick up from where you left off, and carry on as before. God calls us to be resilient followers.

I once helped a man whose business had failed. When he first came to me, he was ready to take his own life. Everything seemed hopeless. Not only had he lost all he owned, but he also lost the money invested by his parents and many of his friends. He felt ashamed and responsible for the hardship he had caused. He couldn't face his children, let alone himself.

What can you say to someone in this predicament? Very little, I'm afraid. The failure is devastating and some suffering is inevitable. All you can do is trust that there is enough resilience for him to see some hope in his future and that he will eventually bounce back.

And bounce back he did. Not too many months after, he began to rise to the challenge left by his first failure. "One failure doesn't make a catastrophe," he would say to himself. He began to think about what lessons he could learn from his failure. Hope began to rise again, and a wiser and much more adaptable man launched himself into business again. This time he was successful. In his failure he had become a real person.

"Does it hurt?" asked the Rabbit.

"Sometimes," said the Skin Horse, for he was always truthful. "When you are Real you don't mind being hurt."

"Does it happen all at once, like being wound up," he asked, "or bit by bit?"

"It doesn't happen all at once," said the Skin Horse. "You become. It takes a long time."

Beginning to Be "Real"

Whatever way we look at it, being "real" is exactly what Christ wants us to be. Could I go so far as to suggest that ultimately our ability to be real depends on whether or not we allow Him to be in full control of our lives? How else can we be totally self-accepting? How else can you cut through your self-dishonesty and see your true self? How else can you determine your true value and bring yourself to the place of being willing and able to forgive yourself?

It is God, His Word, and His Spirit that create in us the desire to be honest with ourselves and show us where we can change and where we cannot change but need to be self-accepting. It is God who gives us the ability and reason to change. He gives us a new perspective on ourselves as well as new values, since we can now see life and its problems through His eyes. He gives us a reason to be forgiving. God sets us on the way to becoming real by doing two important things for us.

• *He frees us.* Romans 6:18 (KJV) says "Being then *made free* from sin, ye became the servants of righteousness" (italics added). The freedom to be real is crucial. What good is discovering your true self, as Dr. Carl Rogers advocates (including the experiencing of your feelings and the removal of your masks) if when you have found yourself; you still don't like what you see? You are then only imprisoned by what you have found but don't like.

Even if you are not afraid of yourself, you are still not free. The beauty of the gospel message is that when you have explored every ounce of your being, when all the corners have been illuminated and the total picture of who you are becomes clear, you are then *set fee* to become a *new creation.* You don't have to settle for the old. Trade it, if you will, for the new creation which God offers you.

• *He transforms us.* Romans 12:1, 2 makes this clear. The transformation takes place "by the renewing of your mind." Even as a psychologist I doubt if I can explain all that is implied in this "renewing" of the mind. I know that it can mean a major upheaval and that our values can change drastically. Suddenly we can tell the essentials of life from the nonessentials, so that we don't clutter our emotions with reactions to that which is trivia in God's sight. We establish new priorities so that we change "I ought to . . ." into "I want to . . ." and each unnecessary "I've got to . . ." becomes secondary to "What does *God* want me to do?" We also receive a clearer understanding of our obligations to others.

So, when you are freed and transformed by the life Christ imparts to you, you have laid the essential foundations for becoming real. You now have the potential for becoming all the things that Carl Rogers and others have so clearly identified as being at the heart of a real person. You can become:

• Genuinely authentic
• Openly transparent
• Acceptingly tolerant
• Comfortingly understanding
• Empathically responsive
• Honestly integrated
• Flexibly adaptable

If you examine each of these qualities closely, you will see that they are all aspects of the fruits of the Spirit. The tragedy is that psychotherapists have clients more willing to develop these qualities than the Holy Spirit has obedient and pliable disciples.

"Give me my Bunny!" [the Boy] said. "You mustn't say that. He isn't a toy. He's REAL!"

When the little Rabbit heard that, he was happy, for he knew that what the Skin Horse had said was true at last. The nursery magic had happened to him, and he was a toy no longer. He was Real. The Boy himself had said it.

That night he was almost too happy to sleep, and so much love stirred in his little sawdust heart that it almost burst.

Barriers to Becoming Real

With all the good intentions in the world, you could still end up spending your life in the toy cupboard. What are some of the barriers to becoming real and what can you do about them?

Beliefs and expectations. I am a great believer in the value of stretching one's potential by attempting the "little extra." It is a good exercise for coming to know our limits. "Reach for a star and perhaps you'll catch a cloud" is a good attitude—up to a point. The problem is that some of us reach for stars in another galaxy. We are unrealistic in setting our goals and ambitions, and consequently we set ourselves up for repeated failure. This can have devastating effects on our quest for reality. If the ratio of our failures to our successes is too high, we are liable to become despondent and discouraged, as well as confused about who we really are.

The solution is to trim back your expectations to a more realistic level. You cannot become what you are not—only what you are.

Let me put it another way. If you honestly know yourself well it is easier to set *realistic* goals. If you don't know yourself, you will increase the ratio of failures to successes. You will attempt too much and only become more frustrated and confused. Make it your aim, therefore, to achieve a realistic understanding of yourself.

An unsatisfactory environment. You are not always to blame for what happens to you. Sometimes you are the victim of unfortunate circumstances. You may have made all the right decisions about work, school, relationships, moving, but everything has gone sour. Helplessness sets in and immobilizes you. You don't see a way out of your unsatisfactory situation. It's as if you are paralyzed and cannot move a muscle. You cannot become real under these circumstances, unless you turn defeat into victory and rise above your helplessness.

The first step to reality is to deal with your helplessness. It may mean having the courage to change your situation; it may mean becoming more assertive and claiming your legitimate rights. To become real you must take full responsibility for your life and implement whatever steps you can (no matter how small) to put this responsibility into action. I don't believe God encourages helplessness. He intends that we should rise up, take control, and claim His resources. Sometimes, just taking a very small step can restore the feeling that you are back in control.

> "It takes a long time [to become Real]. Generally, by the time you are Real, most of your hair has been loved off, and your eyes drop out and you get loose in the joints and very shabby. But these things don't matter at all, because once you are Real you can't be ugly, except to people who don't understand."

Summary

We all long to know who are are—to become full, complete persons who are *real* to ourselves and to others. We often hide from our true feelings and depend on our relationships with others for our sense of reality.

Authenticity is best developed under conditions of acceptance, understanding, and genuineness. We can achieve this through our encounters with others, with courage and openness.

A Christian who accepts the basic tenets of God's love and forgiveness is better able to come to terms with himself and is better equipped to cope with the feelings of isolation which are so prevalent today. Authenticity, integrity, and adaptability are developed as we let God release us from our emotional prisons. Life in Christ frees and transforms us and provides the strength to overcome the barriers to becoming real, as we learn to set realistic goals and deal with unsatisfactory conditions in everyday life. Paradoxically, as we abandon ourselves to God, we become more free to realize our full potential.

Additional Reading

1. *The Velveteen Rabbit,* Margery Williams (New York: Doubleday).
2. *On Becoming a Person,* Carl R. Rogers (Boston: Houghton Mifflin).
3. *Why Am I Afraid to Tell You Who I Am?* John Powell (Niles, IL: Argus Communications).
4. *Dropping Your Guard,* Charles R. Swindoll (Dallas: Word Publishing).
5. Ephesians 2.

Epilogue

I began this book by emphasizing that feelings are a part of life. We cannot escape them, though many find ways to circumvent and distort their experience of them. My message has been a simple one—feelings are our friends and they should neither imprison us nor be imprisoned by us. Knowing how to experience them, own up to them, and even control them when necessary is essential to mental and spiritual health—and to emotional freedom.

I have taken you on a journey through some of your emotions. I hope that for most of you it has been an enlightening journey. Perhaps you have discovered new aspects of your personality and identified the mistakes you most commonly make in the realm of your emotions. Hopefully you have moved nearer to your goal of becoming more real, fully human yet fully spiritual, fully emotional yet fully victorious over your emotions. But some of you may be frustrated over your emotional problems, so I would like to close with some remarks which may be helpful.

1. Perhaps you are saying to yourself: *This is too painful. Becoming a real, emotionally free person seems to hurt more than staying as I am.*

This is true. It may well be more hurtful to change than to stay as you are. But the pain is short-lived, and the freedom which follows is well worth the effort. Psychological growing pains are inevitable. It would be nice if our emotional (and our spiritual) growth were continuous and steady from beginning to end. Unfortunately, it comes in irregular fits and starts—often, I suspect, because we resist change and perpetuate self-destructive behavior without realizing what we are doing. If you are aware of a need for change, have the courage to make the change, even if you find it painful to do so. It can be helpful to remember the following:

Don't expect too much of yourself too soon. This is a common mistake, even for those undergoing psychotherapy. There is no quick and easy road to emotional maturity. Be patient with yourself. You have not learned your present behavior patterns overnight, so don't expect them to vanish that quickly.

Don't expect complete success. Some failures are inevitable, and these are just as necessary for psychological growth as are successes. "Failures are to grow by." Failures pinpoint the weak spots and show where defenses need to be strengthened. On the other hand, don't be content with your failures, but use them as important learning experiences to make the necessary adjustments and corrections to your present behaviors.

Don't become discouraged. Keep experimenting with the ideas I have outlined and find new strategies more applicable to your life situation where necessary. You will often feel most discouragement just before the breakthrough to success—so remember this before you allow your discouragement to cause you to give up.

2. Perhaps you are saying to yourself: *I think I'm better off staying as I am—in my emotional shell.*

A client recently began to risk changing her behavior and relating to her friends in a more authentic, loving, emotionally real way. One little incident backfired and didn't work out just as she expected, so she panicked and pulled back into her emotional shell. "I'll just not trust anyone again. It's *safer* that way," she told me. It took me many sessions to get her back to the point of willingness to take a risk in giving love to others. Eventually she did succeed. Try and try again. True, it may seem safer to stay as you are, but in the long run you will have your reward. Trust God to give you courage to keep trying.

3. Perhaps you are saying to yourself: *It's all very well for more capable and competent people—they can change and become emotionally real. I just don't have what it takes.*

It's possible, I suppose, for some to have read through this book and still have a defeatist attitude. However, I would be more concerned if you felt overly confident to do everything I have outlined by yourself. To feel a measure of inadequacy is more normal than to feel fully competent.

One of the central tenets of the Christian faith is that as human beings we are basically inadequate. It is a delusion to think that we—in ourselves—are totally competent to achieve emotional healthiness. We need God in our lives, and real freedom only comes from total surrender to the living God as helpless, dependent persons. This is the paradox of our humanity. The more dependent we are on God, the more freedom we experience to be ourselves fully.

So in all you seek to do for yourself—for every exercise of loving, for every act of coping with your anger or depression, for every thought controlled and channeled toward constructive emotions—trust and depend on God. Abandon yourself to Him, and you will be freed to fulfill all the potential that is in you.

This is real freedom!